Provenance: Tales from a Bookshop

Provenance

Tales from a Bookshop

Anne M Scriven

K&B

Kennedy & Boyd

Kennedy & Boyd
an imprint of
Zeticula Ltd
The Roan,
Kilkerran,
KA19 8LS
Scotland.

http://www.kennedyandboyd.co.uk
admin@kennedyandboyd.co.uk

First published in 2015

Copyright © Anne M. Scriven 2015
Cover photographs © Sam.Scriven@me.com 2015

ISBN 978-1-84921-146-8

In memory of Michael Martin Connor
26.01.1995 — 24.01.2013,
a lover of books and bookshops.

A chield's amang you takin notes,
And faith [s]he'll prent it.
— Robert Burns, (1789)

A note on the text

These tales are textured with Scots language and therefore, for the confusit, a basic Scots - English glossary has been provided at the end of this book. May I also say to the folks who designed a spell-checker which continually made a total slaister of my words whenever I persisted in the use of Scots — thank you, but it would have been so much the easier without you.

Acknowledgements

GB — for taking on a disillusioned academic; for daring to run a quality bookshop in an unpopular place and in the internet age; for staging a business on a model unknown to any school of marketing; for the volleys of superb flyting, hours of entertainment and quiet kindnesses.

Peter McCormack — who knows his quarto from his verso.

Terry, Michael and Stephanie Connor — who gracefully gave permission for me to record in the chapter 'The Learned Shall Shine' some of the beautiful life force of their beloved son and brother.

Adele Simpson, Linda McMahon, John McGowne and Terry McCribbens — who allowed me to share memories of their remarkable young pupil and friend.

Sam — who keeps me informed of what the cool people are reading, who reminds me of the importance of the happiness factor and who freely gifted some superb cover photographs.

Colum — my astute and reliable first reader who believes both in the bookshop and in the wisdom of leaving some words unsaid.

And finally to all those who unknowingly contributed to this *sui generis* of vignettes, sketches and tales — thank you so much for refusing to entertain the thought that the main function of a bookshop is to sell books. Please don't change, remain exactly as you are, unencumbered by boring conventionality.

Contents

Preliminaries

There are other books about second-hand bookshops. The stories they relate are witty, they make us smile and tut at the daftness of people and the stupid things they say — other people of course, none of us, we would never be so silly. Stories of second-hand bookshops are thus often stories of eccentricity — for only a singular type of person would take on a business which, at best, is destined in this day and age of internet shopping, to do no more than break-even if lucky. The scenes and sketches I have collated here from 'Cloisters Bookshop' are in as much no different from other contributors to the genre. But — and there is a huge BUT involved here — there is one considerable difference between the stories born out of the bookshop I know very well and those I have read about. The difference lies in where the shop is and has its being.

Typically we are unsurprised to find a second-hand bookshop in a wealthy area of a city close to a university or in a bijou square in a cute market town. We think little of finding one in perhaps a 'Crafts n Coffee' farm steading or in a place known as 'a book town' or indeed on a picturesque pier or in a tranquil hamlet in a rural area. Yes, we expect this, delight in it, but are unsurprised. Cloisters, however, exists in none of these alluring settings. You will find it instead, should you set your heart to 'Bold and Brave', in a dingy part of an old West of Scotland town which is hanging on to its once proud identity with its fingertips. The street sign opposite the shop door hangs crooked, the police patrol regularly and regard it is a 'flash area'. Many local residents have pallid skins and social problems. It is increasingly becoming an area of mixed races as new immigrants begin on the bottom rung of the economic ladder. Unemployment and health issues are high, the pubs and local bookies do a good trade. Small independent shops, after an initial burst of enthusiasm, often founder and go bust. First time customers, dropping off books, worry about where to leave their car. In this depressing maelstrom, where three streets merge, sits Cloisters Bookshop.

Cloisters is a large three windowed shop without, much to the amazement of many, grilled protective bars or iron shutters. It is instead fronted by two old wooden storm doors which are hooked open to let the light stream through the interior glassed door. The outside walls are painted white, the windows cleaned regularly and four hanging baskets, stuffed with trailing red nasturtiums and lavender in summer and purple heather and cascading pansies in winter, swing happily just above head height from decorative iron brackets. New visitors to the bookshop, if they are intrepid enough to follow the website travel instructions and persevere even when they think all hope is lost, are amazed it exists where it does. Are amazed at its quality and stock of 40,000 volumes. Are surprised at the knowledge of the staff and the mellow coffee-scented atmosphere they find. People of all ages appear to mentally change gear just by the simple act of pushing open the heavy door – with its injunction to 'PUSH HARD!' and the accompaniment of the jangle of the copper bells fixed above the top lock. These first-time visitors to the shop are easy to spot. Having let go of the bronze-plated door handle to allow the door to swing back into place behind them — although, if truth be told, this never quite happens as a defunct mechanism prefers to leave the door a quarter inch open — they then pause, stand transfixed on the coir mat and stare. They stare not because they are unfamiliar with the concept of a bookshop, but because their minds are trying to equate what they have just left outside and what they are now inside. If familiar with her writing, I suspect they would find themselves agreeing with what Virginia Woolf noted of second-hand bookshops in her essay 'Street Haunting' (1930) :

Here we find anchorage in these thwarting currents of being;
here we balance ourselves after the splendours and miseries of
the streets.

And I doubt if there is a day that goes by without someone saying 'I've often driven past this place and today I've finally made the time to come and investigate.' We usually nod our heads, smile, briefly tell them the layout of the shop and then wait for the stock questions of 'How long have youse been here then?' and 'Are youse the same people who owned the one near the Abbey?' and 'Is it going alright then?' and then the incredulous statement following a sweep of the eyes round the various alleys and nooks, 'Jings, you've a few books here!' These folk then take a meander around the shop in an almost silent veneration as if, by breathing too hard or speaking too loudly, the scene will shimmer before their eyes and fade back into their imagination. What I think people really want to say is 'Man, it's real. It's really real. An authentic second-hand bookshop here, all around me, I can touch it, smell it. And it actually exists. Here!' It is rare though that this is expressly said, because what lies underneath such wonder is the unspoken doubt that such a quality establishment manages to prevail in the area it does. To utter that somehow seems impolite, rude, a bit supercilious. So they bite their lips and continue tip-toeing around the aisles.

They are quite right though. The setting of Cloisters is remarkable and the customer base thus engendered is further remarkable and of a different mix, I jalouse, than any other second-hand bookshop. It is not that the customers described in other books are more literate than those who frequent Cloisters — the following tales will set you straight on that score — but their lives can be, quite literally, streets apart. Being then both a valiant and unique enterprise, the stories I have been privileged to gather are also unique. There are tales here that will, I hope, make you smile, perhaps even laugh. There are tales which may encourage you to ponder and work out your own thoughts on the matter. There are tales which may help you change your belief that all we do in a bookshop is sit behind a counter and read books (wish). There are tales which speak of the broader workings of the secondhand book trade and its relationship to the modern-day publishing world. There are tales which edge near the rueful and poignant. And there is a particular tale which is sad. The story of young Michael Connor was the hardest to write — for reasons which you will understand — but it is Michael's story which stands as testament that establishments such as Cloisters have lasting value and we will be fools to let them disappear.

The vast majority of names of real people, including that of the actual bookshop, have been changed in fairness to those who innocently chatted or performed in front of me. The boundary between fact and fiction thus usefully blurred by this sleight of hand, provides me with a sporting chance of being able to assure the affrontit and pit oot that any resemblance was but that of sheer coincidence. And may I say to those who may recognise something of themselves in these pages, I could perhaps have told you all to be more careful — but then you would have done, and would not have been your individual selves who are most worthy of being recorded for posterity in a book.

Any real names retained — such as Michael's and members of his family — have been retained as permission was sought and kindly granted. Names of authors cited, both living and dead, are also real as they like the fame and they, or their literary executors, could create a right stooshie if I didn't put their actual name with their books.

While fully aware that writing can only ever be a construction, or a provisional précis, I have thus attempted to lay before you a flavour of what happens in Cloisters. Should you wish to sample the full truth you will need to come in and throw yourself into the haill clanjamfrie, safe in the knowledge that I have finished collating stories. Well ... then again ...

The Main Protagonist

Forbye its setting, a major idiosyncrasy of Cloisters is its owner — as all who have had the experience of first-hand encounter, must surely agree. As already said, to want to operate, (or perhaps the word 'govern' is more appropriate in this instance), a second-hand bookshop, has always required a distinctive turn of mind. Previous to Kelvin's reign, the business was owned by a woman my husband and I had dubbed 'Aunty Wainwright' — owing both to her rather severe no-nonsense, no haggling, approach to the buying and selling of books and her quirky marketing practices. Those who are still in doubt about our naming of her may perhaps like to watch re-runs or get yourself a box set of the successful BBC series *Last of the Summer Wine* — and you will get the allusion. The current owner is not of this cast but instead it will be useful for you to think more on the lines of another BBC production — that of their adaption of James Herriot's (or Alf Wright's) tales about his life as a 'vetneray' in the Yorkshire Dales as illustrated in the series *All Creatures Great and Small*. Having got this far then study the character of Siegfried Farnon, James Herriot's eccentric boss. In the real life of Alf Wright this was the bombastic but generous-hearted Donald Vaughan Sinclair, enacted superbly in the BBC series by Robert Hardy. Despite the differences in nationality, profession and love of animals, and despite the fact that Siegfried is fond of a drop of good dry sherry and Kelvin is a convinced teetotaller, there is, without argument, much similarity in the infrastructure of both men. Take, for example, the fondness for setting rules, wishes or tasks only to change them a few minutes, hours or days later:

- I don't like biscuits being kept in the shop'... 'Aaaagh, why are there no biscuits?

- It's not a good idea to have coffee while the children's writing class is in'... 'What's happened to the coffee?

- I don't like being pestered by people who want to talk rubbish for ages'... 'Yes, drop back in tomorrow.

- Your priority is to get the table clear of books ...'Right. I've emptied a shelf, can you dust and cull it please then do something with the poetry inventory.

And, famously:

- We're not taking in any more books ... What have you got?

I have to say though that I am totally in favour of the now established Siegfriedesque shop policy of blaming others for what you may have done yourself. That's a rather sound and useful behaviour and one I could happily adopt in other areas of my life.

What must be genuinely lauded however, is the fact that it takes guts to both run a second-hand bookshop in the early twenty-first century with its fascination for all things digital, and secondly to run it where it is. The real Kelvin with his horror of open praise instead of good Scots Calvinist flavoured 'Who do you think y'ur?' and 'Dinna get above yersel' mentality, will pour hellfire scorching scorn over this. In fact he'll pour it all over the book saying something like 'I don't think you've got this place or me accurately at all'. I expect no less. But hey-ho, as I may resign or be asked to leave after publication, I should take the opportunity to tell it as I see it. Otherwise this will become a work of imagination — and, dear reader, it so is not. Oh no.

So let me reiterate. It takes guts to do what Kelvin does where he does it. And the presentation of the shop should also be commended. While the owner of the fruit and veg shop opposite us appears to be content with peeling and scuffed paintwork, Kelvin, every so often has the shop front painted, the hanging baskets refreshed, the windows kept clean, dog-dirt washed away, and has asked about plant troughs being installed on the railings outside the shop. Yes, of course all of that enhances the shop but such practices also enhance the street. Cloisters is then not just a bookshop but also an unselfish public service.

And, as you read on, you will also become aware of how Cloisters is a place that appears to meet the needs of people who, as the wee girl in *Mr God This Is Anna* by Sydney Hopkins realises, have some kind of hole in them. Be it a desire for conversation, a laugh, a banter, a space to air their views on life, a (sometimes) place of thought and quiet, or even somewhere to browse and purchase a book (it does happen), Cloisters offers something other than that found in bland shopping malls with their samey shops and piped musak. It is, quite simply, a place of difference and a place that makes a difference.

Children who visit the shop immediately recognise that they are in a place where things run along divergent lines and 'the man' who seems to be in charge (that is worthy of debate at times), has a way of speaking to them which they haven't yet encountered in a grown-up. Refusing the more commonplace usage of a higher tone, simple language and slight patrony deployed by most adults when addressing young kids, Kelvin instead treats them as independent beings who have thoughts and opinions of their own and, as such, are usually good entertainment. 'Micro Stovie', as Kelvin has dubbed her, is a good example. This is a young lass around eight years of age, who has been named thus due to the fact that her mum, dubbed 'Wee Stovie' because of her neat physique, owns the nearby Stovies Café. Micro Stovie frequents the bookshop most school holidays. She is sent along the street with the purpose of delivering some tasty morsel of food or drink for Kelvin or to search for something to read to keep her occupied in the café while her parent rushes about efficiently serving all and sundry. The 'conversation' between Micro Stovie and Kelvin usually flows something along the lines of:

Oh here, it's Micro Stovie. What you doing here? Why are you not at the school?

Giggle … giggle … It's a holiday.

A holiday. Again! How are you going to get an education if you keep staying off school?

Giggle … giggle … I'm not staying off. It's shut.

That's what you tell your mum. You just want a day off to sit and eat chips and other fattening things in the café.

Giggle … giggle … No I don't. And I don't like chips anyway.

Not like chips? What kind of child are you?

Giggle … giggle …

And what's that in your hand? Coffee? What's wrong with our coffee?

Giggle … giggle … It's hot chocolate.

Ooooh. Coming in here with your posh hot chocolate, spurning our coffee.

Giggle … giggle … I don't like coffee and Mum says hot chocolate is better for me.

I suppose I'll have to give her that. She might just be right. So, are you going to look at the books or are you just going to giggle and keep me from my work?

It was you who started talking to me!

No it wasn't. You came in here and started blethering all kinds of rubbish and I had to join in.

Giggle … giggle … Anyway I know what I want.

That's good, it's always good to know what you want in life. Be definite though, don't keep changing your mind.

Giggle … giggle … I'm not changing my mind. I want this.

That? A book? I thought we were talking about what you are going to do with your life?

Noooo … *giggle …* I just want to buy this book.

Ok. Ok. You can buy it. But you do need to think seriously about your life and what kind of future you want.

I'm only eight! *giggle … giggle.*

Never too early to start planning. Bet that's what your mum did. That's smart. You need to be smart like her'

Giggle … giggle … I am smart! I'm good at school!

How do I know that? You could just be making it up.

I'm not! I'm not! *giggle … giggle.*

Well, when you're sitting with your book and plate of chips this afternoon, have a wee think about what you want to do with your life. A good start would be not to eat so many chips.

Giggle … giggle … I told you I don't like chips!

What a strange child you are. Oh, you're away. Say hi to your mum. Tell her I didn't like the cream of broccoli soup she insisted on giving me yesterday.

But you always tell her to choose a soup for you! You should choose it yourself.

Choose it myself? I'm too busy for that. I have to rely on her choices. Anyway, bye!!

Bye! *giggle … giggle … giggle …*

As you will now understand, where most adults might pass encouraging comment about the child's book choice or style of dress or cute smile etc, Kelvin refrains from such phatic communication and opts instead for the pedagogy of : 'Give me a child before or after the age of seven and I'll totally confuse him or her'. Let me amuse you with another couple of examples:

Kelvin: (*To a woman who has young child around two years old with her*): Send the young man over here.

Customer: Ruaridh, take your book over to the man.

Small customer toddles over and levers his book up onto the counter.

Kelvin: Thank you young man. So, how's your day going?

Small customer: —

Kelvin: When you leave here are you going for your lunch?

Small customer nods.

Kelvin. That's good. It's good to have lunch. What will you have?

Small customer: ——

Kelvin: Oh I see, it's a surprise lunch. Maybe you'll have fish and chips. Do you like fish and chips?

Small customer: ——

Kelvin: No. I can see that you don't. I don't blame you. All that messing about with a knife and a fork. Too fussy. No, you're better off I think with a bowl of porridge. Do you like the parritch?

Small customer: ——

Kelvin: I can recommend it. You know where you are with the parritch. Good solid stuff. Fills you up and there's only a spoon to think of.

Small customer's mother comes over.

Kelvin: Eh, your offspring tells me he would like porridge for his lunch.

Small customer's mother: Really? I don't think he's ever had porridge.

Kelvin: Ah well, he's a man of great discernment and wants porridge.

Small customer's mother: Oh, well porridge it is then. Must say he's never asked for that before.

Small customer: ——

Then there was the short memorable interchange:

Kelvin: How are you today Lauren?

Lauren: Feeling a bit sad.

Kelvin: Why's that?

Lauren: My goldfish died.

Kelvin: Well, at least you know what you're having for your tea tonight.

Lauren: *Waaaah ....*

And then there was ...

Kelvin (*To a young lad*) : Ah young man, young man, what age are you? Are you over twelve?

Boy: No, I'm seven.

Kelvin: Seven. Ok that's fine. And your sister what is she?

Boy: She's one.

Kelvin: That's no good. One disnae count.

Boy: —

Kelvin: So, do you know of any good names for spiders?

Boy: How about...

Kelvin: *Mmmm.* Interesting name. 'Howabout'

Boy: No, that's not the name!

Kelvin: Changed your mind already? Ok, have another go. What name for our spider?

Boy: Have you got a spider?

Kelvin: Obviously.

Boy: Where is it?

Kelvin: In our window. Duh!

Boy looks towards the window.

Boy: That spider?

Kelvin: Yes. Yes. What other spider is there?

Boy: Do you want me to give it a name?

Kelvin: I've already said so. Are you a slow learner?

Boy. *Mmmm.* How about...

Kelvin: You've already said that. I thought you didn't want that name?

Boy: NO! THAT'S NOT THE NAME!

Kelvin: You're obviously getting in a muddle. You're leaping in too quickly. Have a good long think then write it down on this piece of card. Ask your mum if you can put your phone number down and if your name comes out of the hat on Halloween we will phone you up — make sure your wee sister doesn't answer or that will confuse things — and you may have won a prize.

Boy: What's the prize?

Kelvin: How do I know? I only own this shop.

And then there's Zach – one of our much more regular young visitors who takes Kelvin and his ways in his sanguine stride. For example:

It's four o'clock on a dark winter afternoon. The door bells clink as a bed-headed secondary school boy enters. Jacket open, tie askew, face flushed with fast movement or the effort to lug his huge backpack which hangs on straps too far extended from his small square shoulders. He trogs up to the counter, sends me a lop-sided smile and makes his way over to the table.

'Zach,' I say, putting down my pile of Ladybird First Readers. 'How's it going?'

'S'alright,' he says, crashing his bag down and flopping onto a seat. 'Phew. Double PE ...!'

'Double PE — that's abuse,' I say.

He grins.

Kelvin emerges from the back corridor.

'Boy! What? What? Why are you not at the school?'

'It's finished,' Zach says.

'Finished! Finished! It's the middle of the afternoon! '

Zach rolls his eyes and unzipping his bag begins to pull out some jotters and a very tatty looking book.

'Is it ok if I do my Maths homework? Ma mum isn't home yet.'

'Sure thing,' I say 'but don't ask me anything — took me three times to get a Maths 'O' Grade.'

'Yes. Don't ask her. She's totally dim. Cannae count. You should see the mess she makes of the till. Just cannae get the staff. Just cannae get the staff,' Kelvin chunters.

Zach rolls his eyes again, jams open his book by flattening it on the table upside down and smoothing it with what looks like a rather grimy fist, then says 'Oh, can I phone ma mum to let her know I'm here?'

'Thought you said she wasn't in yet? You're getting confused. It's all that jumping over wooden horses in the gym, goes to the head,' says Kelvin.

Zach ignores him and comes over to the counter. I hand him the phone. He dials and after a moment says 'Hi mum, it's me. Ah'm in the bookshop. Love you.'

'Just the answer machine,' he says handing the phone back to me and trotting back to the table.

'Do you want a drink of water,' I ask. Memories of my son arriving home from school swim into my mind. A big drink was always on the 'Need Now' list.

'Yes please,' says Zach, 'if it's no bother.'

Somehow there is an echo of an adult voice in that, but it's still charming.

'No bother at all,' I say. 'Or maybe you'd like tea? It's a wee touch freezin today.'

'Aw. That would be great,' he says, his big brown eyes twinkling at the thought.

'Don't give him tea!' says Kelvin 'he's here to do his homework. How's he going to be a top brain surgeon if you keep distracting him with tea?'

I roll my eyes at Zach who presses his lips together suppressing a laugh. Make tea in a proper cup, add lots of milk — resulting in what we used to call 'dinky tea' — put it down in front of him as well as a Tunnock's Tea Cake — our second national biscuit after shortbread.

'Yes!' he grins and tucks in, swinging his legs happily.

I wink at him then let him get on with his snack and his homework.

After some fifteen minutes he shuts his jotter and jams it with the book back into his bag.

'Done,' says.

'Done? Done?' says Kelvin. 'What are your teachers thinking? What about all the other stuff?'

'What stuff?' says Zach

'The German. The English. The Science.' says Kelvin.

'We didn't get any homework for that,' says Zach.

'Pathetic. Pathetic. They're obviously making your school experience enjoyable. Don't they know you're supposed to hate it?' says Kelvin disappearing again down the back corridor.

Zach giggles then asks. 'Is my book around?'

'There you go,' I say giving him a Darren Shan novel from the pile behind the counter.

'Thanks,' he says and settles back at the table for a good read.

I watch him turn the pages, and wonder for the umpteenth time, how many children there are in today's world that is becoming so devoid of bookshops, who have access to this kind of place? How many children are there who know a bookshop really well, who have one at the bottom of their street, who are so familiar with it that they take it for granted? I wonder if in years hence, when all most people will know of the printed word is that of the electronic format, will Zach tell people of his childhood and preface many a story with 'There was this weird bookshop...', and he will move his mind back to these hours and remember them as rather magical. Or just totally off-beat? Maybe we'll end up in his book. Wonder what names he'll give us?

Being the smart lad he is though he has also realised that sometimes some protection is required if one is to get any kind of peace. Of late he has taken to nipping home before he comes into the bookshop, dumping his school stuff, emptying his schoolbag of all contents and replacing them with his big black laptop, power cable and — most importantly — a rather large set of headphones. We have discovered however that although the headphones give off the impression of I'm-in-the-zone-man-so-there-is-no-point-talking-to-me, Zach can actually hear all that is going on around him. I tested this out by asking him in a normal level of voice if he would like a Blue Riband biscuit. He nodded vigorously and thanked me politely. Three minutes later however when Kelvin hurled a veiled insult about twelve year old lads' non-commitment to hard study that would further their ambitions to be fluent in five languages, Zach blinked but kept his eyes on the screen. Seems that outsize headphones come with filtered hearing. And, heh, what a good idea – I mean, really! Maybe personal headphones should be *de rigueur* safety equipment for second-hand bookshop workers. The subliminal message to all around to quit pestering you with their rubbish and let you get on with what you want to get on with, is worth its weight in gold or at least the price of a natty set of headphones. I may invest in some. I don't mind looking like a middle-aged Princess Leia if it accords me the luxury of not having to answer daft questions or to look remotely interested. *Hmmm.* Sometimes kids just get it right.

To be a Writer

There are the kids who regularly come to the bookshop not to do their homework, drink tea, play computer games using the WiFi or to have a laugh with Kelvin. These kids are those who form the excellent Young Writer's Club and who willingly tumble out of their warm beds most Saturday mornings, forsake a tempting slump in front of the telly in their Onesie in company with generous bowls of cereal, and instead opt for a brain-teasing, mind-stretching creative session at the bookshop. It is perhaps typical that these kids don't need the writer's club for additional help with their literacy — from what I overhear their literacy is in superb working order — but instead come to the club (a) because it's fun and (b) because even at their young age, they've realised that words are what make the world go round. And they like the setting. It's quirky. It's authentic. It's different. I have heard them speculate if there is a ghostly spectre in 'the spooky corridor' — which apparently necessitates them going in twos to the kitchen if they need to wash sticky hands. Or if there is a secret lever behind one of the bookcases which, when pulled, will reveal a dust laden room where ancient scrolls, various caskets of priceless jewellery and a suspicious goblin reside. I hope they keep me posted on that one.

They are more than ably led by Rosie, a young cherry-cheeked, bouncy-haired woman, often supported by her lieutenant, Diana, a smiling calm presence who quietly helps implement Rosie's ideas. As I work around the shop while the group is in session, I silently applaud how Rosie deftly manages her young charges with a seemingly endless creative headful of interesting exercises and games. Should the noise-level begin to intrude on other browsing customers in the shop, Rosie reigns in her excitable squad with some intriguing puzzle or writerly exercise. I have yet to hear her issue any reprimand or quelling stare. Such traditional teacherly norm just doesn't come into her methods. In defence of classroom teachers I should quickly say that it is perhaps precisely because Rosie isn't a trained teacher, or more to the point, isn't the class teacher of any of the kids in her care, isn't running her group in a school, isn't attempting to deal with a class size of thirty or more pupils and isn't following any constricting national curriculum, that her group relate to her the way they do and it runs as successfully as it does. Perhaps the major difference is that the children opt to come, it's their decision, their desire.

The setting is a major contributing factor too. The environment of shelves and shelves of books, an old wooden table with five sturdy oak chairs, the quiet chug of the coffee machine and its ensuing aroma, the sound of pages being flicked over by other bookshop users, the *ping!* of the till, the sudden laughter in response to a Kelvinesque joust, the musical rattle of the door chimes, the sound of books tumbling to the floor, all quietly seeps into their senses and generates an alternative behaviour where they want to create words, want to spill out the thoughts in their heads, and want to write.

The bookshop staff don't interfere with the group unless to meet a request for water, direct where the hand-drier for the loo is, help find a required resource book or, as can happen, clean dog-dirt off the shoe of an embarrassed youngster. But we get to listen and to quietly smile at the enunciated thoughts of young minds. We also get to read the published culmination of a term's work as each year Rosie organises a printed booklet made up of the best pieces constructed by the group. The production of the booklet acts as an excellent incentive to get the words out there and to be the best ones possible. The booklet boasts the young folks' skill and ease with various genres — the traditional storyline, memoir, haiku, collaborative plot lines, storyboarding and brief screenplays, to name but some. I expect these kids will need little help when it comes to writing their reflective styled essays as part of their Higher English course — which they will probably all be capable of passing at least two years before the usual age. I often hear Rosie encourage the kids by saying 'Don't worry about spelling, just get your ideas down'. This is time honoured advice. Dorothea Brande in her landmark book *Becoming a Writer* (1934), a text which is often required reading for any student of Creative Writing, stresses (or dictates) that to get better at writing, to achieve anything in the writing world, you must write, write and write. I find the tone of Brande's book a little narky and perjink for my taste but agree nonetheless, (as if she would care), with her advice that on the first impulse, while letting the words out, the writer shouldn't stop to question how correct or grammatical they are, but just let them out. Get the words flowing first and employ the spell-checker later — or red pen as it would have been in Brande's time. She also goes on about being really strict about when you will write and committing to it come hell or high water. Guess that's also good advice unless you are the one dealing with the moaning plumber, the belligerent gas man, the shopping, the cooking, the cleaning, the dogs, your other job/s and the significant people in your life. I prefer the gentler, more compassionate, less judgmental and more persuasive zen wisdom of Natalie Goldberg, author of *Writing Down the Bones: Freeing the Writer Within* (1986), who says that it is only by being sensitive and aware of the language running in your mind that good writing will happen. Fortunately, being kids and not yet into the terrible 'Should' of the adult psyche, the young writers' group appear to take delicious pleasure in their weekly writing session, scribbling freely and furiously, then flinging down their pencil, saying 'Wait till you hear this, it's fab!'

I also get high amusement from overhearing their zest for fun cranking up as the session goes on.

'What's a good name for a dog?' asks one.

'Eric,' replies another, to gales of laughter.

Or,

'Listen everyone,' chirps a lass. 'I stepped on a cornflake this morning — does that make me a serial killer?'

And,

'Hey, I've thought of a great idea … how about whoopee *shoes* instead of a whoopee cushion! Imagine that. *Faaart … faaart … faaart … faaart …*' (Oh, no, sorry, that one was my husband's idea, but he was talking to a nine year old at the time.)

Anyway, the kids are just great. I hope they keep their superb nose for mischief and still get a laugh from their writing when they're older. Refuse all that tormented angst that the famous seem to feed on with their 'deeply disturbing dark tale' and 'profoundly upsetting plot lines' and all that fashionable *noir* which all writers of the genre think so unique but has actually been scribbled to death, and instead write something that makes their readers laugh from the bottom of their bellies. I'd buy it. As Elizabeth Jane Howard said of the perky observational novels of Elizabeth Von Arnim, the sustained but not overplayed happiness inscribed in books such as *The Enchanted April* — (published in 1922, an *annus mirabilis* in the literary world, when the joys of Eliot's 'Wasteland' and Joyce's *Ulysses* also appeared … thanks for those boys, they're a romping cheery read) — is harder to write of than its reverse and is a mark of a quality writer. Or, as Miss Austen asserted in *Mansfield Park* :

> *Let other pens dwell on guilt and misery. I quit such odious subjects as soon as I can, impatient to restore everybody not greatly in fault themselves to tolerable comfort, and to have done with all the rest.*

And if you miss doom and gloom, feel free to listen to any news broadcast any time any day.

So the young writers' class, in my book (hey, literally!), is a definite plus to have in the shop. It has also worked well for me on a slightly more personal level. While either depositing or collecting their creative offspring some of the parents potter around the shop a bit. If Kelvin hasn't got me up to the eyes in other tasks I tend to chat a bit with the lurking parents. They know that that bookshop staff aren't involved in the running of the writers' class so our blethers tend to run on other lines. I get on well with Carolyn, one of the mums. She's a calm and intelligent woman and besides that, she was kind enough to buy not one but two copies of my last book — ok, it is on prominent display in the shop and I lose no opportunity to shamelessly boost it to customers, particularly if they are unfortunate to mention anything about dogs — but not all verbal bludgeoning of customers results in an actual sale. Carolyn's kindness then further extended to posting a flattering review on Amazon (blatant hint … blatant hint…) and to bringing into the shop two friends who were visiting from New Zealand.

One of these friends was Peter Farrell whom Carolyn wanted me to meet as Peter had recently published a memoir — *The Lie That Settles* — which recounts his experience of growing up not knowing he had a living father and the subsequent tracing of him and his step brother and sister. Peter told me that he had been interviewed on radio in New Zealand and on his way home was stopping off to do a reading at the Auckland Writers' Festival where he was sharing a platform with none other than Janice Galloway. My envious writer's heart lurched a bit at that — Janice Galloway belongs to the far off promised land of 'Established Writer', so I jaloused that Peter's book must be good stuff. We blethered a bit about the minefield that is life-writing and swapped stories of where we had both stepped on one. How do you write about what you see, feel, taste, hear, remember, and who you encounter in all of that, without offending and simultaneously being faithful to your understanding and the workings of literary cohesion? Neither Peter nor myself had a useful answer to that because, unless you stick to mentioning people who are dead and who have absolutely no living descendants, then the memoir writer is undoubtedly going to dischuff someone along the way — even, if for the fact that they didn't get a mention. I advised Peter to read Gerard Durrell's introduction to his *Birds, Beasts and Relatives* (1969), where, in response to his family who had dictated that on no account was he to write about them ever again, he felt there was only one course of action open to him — i.e. to write some more. They can always get you back anyway by composing a death march in your honour on your birthday or something.

The upshot of a our natter was that Peter took a copy of my last book and promised to send me a copy of his memoir. Zipedeedodah! First sale in New Zealand! A week or so later I received an email from Peter saying that he had read my book, saying some nice things about it, and that he had posted it on to his daughter in Dubai. Double Zipedeedodah! First sale (sort of) in the Middle East! My wee book about our nutty rescue dog, is turning out to be a real trekker. I think of the genial parson, Mr Beebe, in Forster's *Room With A View* (1908), delighting in the travels of the slight but pertinacious Miss Alans whom, he believes, will end up going right round the world. On the wings of kind authors, friends, and families of friends, it looks like my book may just do that. Yeh! Yeh young writers club! Thanks for your help. (And Peter did send his book — it's good, read it.)

Fechtin Books

It is curious to me that the Military History section constantly attracts men of middle age and upwards who want not only to search for a book, possibly to buy or order another, but to tell us at length what the book is about. They are fond of openers such as 'This is a fantastic book — it tells you the real story of the SAS / Hitler's think tank/ the Cold War / The Gulf War / Iraq / the IRA' ... the examples are endless. What they really mean of course is that the said book offers a window to an experience they have not had but think thrilling and incredible. History, for them, is solely a linked series of invasions, battles, conflicts, treaties, revolutions. Any deviation from this linear narrative comes under the specialist subject of Conspiracy Theory — which, invariably turns out to be a euphemism for their own personal take on things. A personal take which they are again only too delighted to share with us.

That history could include discussion on how people (which usually means women) got on with care and continuance of daily existence through the ages while the men were beating the hell out of each other, is dismissed, if thought of at all, as completely irrelevant and in the bracket of 'Not History'. As Virginia Woolf (yes, I know I've already quoted her, but so? so?) astutely argued in her essay 'Women and Fiction' (1929):

> The history of [the world] is the history of the male line, not of the female. Of our fathers we know always some fact, some distinction. They were soldiers or they were sailors; they filled that office or they made that law. But of our mothers, our grandmothers, our great-grandmothers, what remains?

I am reminded here of something I saw in the 1980s while visiting my sister who was setting up a Primary Health Care unit in Sierra Leone. This was pre Civil War and Ebola — what medical help or intervention that country needs now is possibly immeasurable. During our visit to my sister's temporary home in Mongobendugu, a local woman walked past one morning with what appeared to be half a tree on her head. While she had been out busting a gut to get firewood for the next few days, her brave warrior man could be seen quietly sleeping under a tree. When I asked my sister why he wasn't helping his wife, she replied 'Oh, he can't. He's waiting for war.'

Why women's contribution to history has always been under-represented is however a thesis for another day. And that thesis will not be written by the chaps who hang out around our Military History shelves searching for adventure and affirmation of their assumptions.

It was therefore rather thought provoking when a mid-thirtyish man came into the shop late one afternoon wearing an arty fusion of a University of Cambridge scarf, a vintage trench coat, skinny jeans, brown leather brogues and flat eight-piece tweed cap and, in an educated Scots voice, asked my advice about recreational reading material — I think he actually called it that. After a bit of probing on my part he let slip he was an army officer home on leave.

'I'm presuming then that you don't want to indulge in a busman's holiday kind of reading?' I said gesturing at our Military History shelves.

He shuddered. 'No. Definitely not. I want something else. Something funny but well written, and nothing to do with my day job.'

'Jerome — *Three Men in a Boat*? Compton Mackenzie — *Whisky Galore*? Lillian Beckwith — *Beautiful Just!*? some Saki? or Crompton — her William books? Or something more contemporary?'

'Oh, good calls, the old favourites will do fine. Do you have any of those?'

He left a half hour later, on his way to 'supper', with three copies of *Three Men in a Boat* as found in our New But Cheap shelves, a Folio edition of stories by Saki, two battered but readable paperback volumes by Compton Mackenzie and a couple of Buchans. All of which he said he would be posting to friends on active service.

Funny old world isn't it? The chaps who aren't fighting want to read about it. The chaps who are, don't. Apparently though this is quite usual behaviour. Writing that focused on overt domestic detail and social intrigue — such as that which flowed from the pen of Jane Austen — was highly desired by soldiers in the trenches during the WWI who wanted their minds to be taken far away from their immediate reality. My own father, while enduring what had to be endured in the five long years as a POW in Poland during WWII, often said the adventures of Zane Grey, cowboy extraordinaire, did much to keep his sanity within reach.

Perhaps though the urge to attack and dominate is hard for the simple mortal to resist? I say this because I am aware that I wage my own private war on the Military History section. To my mind there is just too much of it. If the adage 'You are what you read' is in any way true then it seems to me that the world could do with much less focus on people wishing to hurl bullets and bombs at each other — and particularly those who order others to do so. Yes of course evil must be stopped, but are we really no further forward than the answer of brute force? I have long held the imaginative fantasy that when a world leader sketches out his plan to invade a country not his to invade and take what is not his to take and put the lives of hundreds of young men at risk while he himself remains in safety, then a couple of experienced infant nursery workers should appear by his side, calmly take his microphone, mobile phone and gun away, lead him to a quiet room, close the door and tell him he is not getting a snack until he says he is ready to be good boy and play nicely. I can think of a few women I know who would be up for the job. Would make a nice break from their usual more demanding charges.

But improbable fantasies aside, when working on the Military History section I enjoy deploying my own counter attack on the masses of shelved books stretching over three metres wide — and that doesn't include the small mountains of books stacked on the floor. I haven't as yet managed to do much with the highest shelves where outsize books reside. This is because (a) our stable health-and-safety advised footstool or 'elephant's foot' as it has been christened, is often needed elsewhere in the shop and (b) there is only so much I can ask my middle-aged shoulders, neck muscles and arms to do. After only twenty minutes of stretching up to dislodge books, dust or discard and rearrange, I feel as if I have done the equivalent of thirty press-ups — an activity I never could get the hang or purpose of. Slow progress has therefore been made of the higher echelons of the section.

My carefully plotted offensive has also to be carried out when Kelvin is out of the shop. I don't want to see him wail as I trot past on my way to the recycle boxes carrying a heap of bound paper that has lain unread on the shelves for too long a time. I mean just how many volumes of *The Memoirs of Field Marshal Montgomery* do we need? Or that series of *Forgotten Voices* — best I think to go with the hint in the title and let them slide into oblivion. And as to the gun-wielding muscled and black balaclavad chaps who seem to like their photos on the front cover of books, as any mum would tell you, it is best not to give them too much attention and I enjoy dropping extraneous copies into the recycle boxes — I swear I can hear them rage as I do so. But it upsets Kelvin and, like the rest of the staff, have learned not to openly flaunt my secret culling strategies. Or, if questioned why I have put two hulking tomes of *The Real Story of WWII in Grisly and Graphic Pictures* in the recycle box, I have learned to adopt a snippy tone and say 'There are another two of the same already out,' in much the same way as I suspect Kelvin's long suffering wife might answer. He tends to go quiet then and I can get on with more necessary decimation and quickly seal up the boxes with their fractious prisoners squashed together inside. This is definitely a section of the shop where decisive and deft action is necessary if the threatening anarchy, continuous revolution and smouldering *coup d'état* is to be quashed.

Jist Crabbit

Thin mean looking kind of chap. The type that has always been old and tetchy. Looks like a Lemony Snicket character. Probably only in his late sixties or early seventies but the twist of his features makes him seem around ninety. Wears old men clothes, threadbare tweed type, worn out cotton, not, I judge, because of poverty or shabby-chic style, just meanness. Asks if we have any collections of fairy tales. I show him the books above the children's section where we keep such things. Today there are roughly eight different editions and volumes — one large Grimms, two World, two Victorian, one Scottish, one Irish, one Australian — Australian? He looks up pursing his draw-string pale lips.

'Just the one Grimms?' he says. 'I would have thought you would have had more than that.'

'They come and go,' I reply. 'We get asked for fairy tales quite often, they seem popular. We did have the paperback edition of Philip Pullman's *Grimm Tales for Young and Old* even though it's quite recently published, but that no sooner reached the shelf than it was bought.'

'Aye, but I thought you would have had more than that,' he whines again.

I look at his liverish face as he peers upwards at the books and see a little boy. A little boy who finds life irksome because those around won't do exactly as he wishes. I wonder why this is. What it was he lacked early in life? Whatever it is our selection of fairy tales obviously isn't going to offer resolution.

'Well, that's all we have today,' I say in the same quiet but firm tone I would use to a small tired child and begin to move off.

'I thought you would have had more,' he says for the third time.

The compassionate analyst in me gets jostled out of the way by my west of Scotland 'nae messin' mentality.

'What are you, the fairytale police?' I say.

He gazes at me open-mouthed, looks back up at the books and mutters, quietly, 'I just thought'.

When Push comes to Shove

A dark haired forty-something chap walks towards me where I sit at the desk pricing Haynes manuals. There is a large canvas hold-all hanging from his right shoulder. His eyes don't sweep the gauntlet of bookshelves as the walks towards me. A man with a mission. A man with a selling mission if I'm not mistaken.

'Hallo there,' I say.

'Hallo,' he replies. 'Do you buy books?'

I'm not mistaken and my heart thuds down two notches. Of all the tasks involved in my job this is the one I like least. I sometimes think we should have a print-out of our philosophy on buying books which we would give to the customer, and tell them to sit down and read, before continuing the process. It would certainly save a lot of time. But books, like people, are often individuals and so perhaps formatting a rule-of-thumb would be difficult but it would still save me from doing The Script. And Kelvin has gone out on a house clearance and I don't expect him back. I'm going to have to deal with this one on my own. I pray he has a bag full of mainstream thrillers which are easy-peasy to price or reject.

'Have you sold books in here before?' I ask.

'No,' he says as he levers his bag off his shoulder, drops it to the ground, bends over and begins to unzip it. Quick action is needed.

'In that case you need to know the following,' I say to his bent back.

He straightens up and I elucidate:

'For paperbacks in good condition we pay around 30p, for hardbacks around 50p — provided we don't already have them in stock and think we can sell them on.'

His mouth forms into a small smirk. Bad sign. Usually means the customer thinks he knows better.

'I think you might need to pay me a lot more for these,' he says.

'Well, let me see,' I say.

Stage One of The Script hasn't worked. We're on to Stage Two.

He lifts out four to five slim hardbacks. Around ten aviation, four Churchill, two motorcycle, ten adventure story. I pick up one of the aviation volumes.

'Specialist books,' I say.

He likes this word.

'Yes, I think they may be worth something. You probably won't have had these in here before.'

'Maybe yes, maybe no,' I rejoin. He is definitely on the 'I know better than you' track.

The books are old — as in thirty to fifty years old — in good condition with only slight wear and tear. I flick through one, no markings, that's good. But there are multiple questions in my head. Do we need them? What are they worth? What can we pay? Do we want them? This is not going to be a simple process. My shrinking soul wishes that Kelvin were here but I tell myself not to be cowardly and deal with it. But I need time to think. The shop is quiet, which is good, I can claim the time.

'I'm going to do some checking on the internet,' I say. 'Then I'll show you the results.'

Possibly contrary to other businesses Kelvin advocates that it is always best to show your thinking to the customer. If they don't like the result at least they know how we have arrived at it. Customers often believe that the shop is rolling in cash and that we will coolly grab hold of an offered book, pay a paltry price for it, and then sell it for hundreds at an auction somewhere. Wish. Were that the case the staff wouldn't be on minimum wage, Kelvin would claim a wage, the shop would be situated somewhere other than where it is and we would do more than just break-even each month. This however isn't the time to do that bit of The Script. No, this is 'The Internet Does Not Lie' bit.

The chap is pleased I'm giving his books time. He picks up a soft bound book with a pen and ink drawing of some kind of light aircraft on the front.

'I think this one alone will be quite valuable,' he says.

Yes, he's definitely on the 'they can afford to pay me lots' belief. I don't comment as I am typing in another title hoping that the page I am on will suffice to illustrate my points. The book comes up as being worth £2.50. I swing the monitor round and say 'As you can see here, this isn't worth much'.

'But more than 50p,' he says.

'Yes, but we can only offer a fifth of the going price, this is a business after all. And you always have the option of taking them away and trying somewhere else,' I say, employing Stage Three and remembering to smile.

'Is there another bookshop near here?' he asks.

'No,' I reply and pick up another book.

Perhaps put off a little he says 'Em, I'll leave you to check another couple and look round a bit.'

I murmur assent as I am now double checking another book on aviation. This one is averaging around £50 on Amazon. Not that that means a lot — there are a lot of chancers out there. I check another. This one is around £30. So, a mixed bag indeed. Time for Stage Four. I go and find the chap who is now hovering in the Thriller corridor.

'Might be best if you come and see this for yourself,' I say.

At the counter I show him the results on screen.

'Your best bet is to take these home and sell them privately. As you can see you may be able to get a lot more than we can offer. But, a word of caution, even though they are coming up at this price it doesn't mean to say that they will sell.'

The ball is now back in his court. What he wants of course is for me to say that I will offer to buy the books for at least a couple of hundred. That I am not about to do unless I don't want paid this month.

'I'll maybe do that,' he says, 'but what about the Churchills? I could leave them with you but I would want at least a pound for each.'

He doesn't get it. We like *non*-pushy people. If he said a softer thing like 'Would you like the Churchills?' I might then offer him a slightly higher price for them than 50p. I have however another strategy for this situation. I leave the desk and walk over to the Military History wall. I open my arms to encompass a shelf which clearly says 'Churchill'. Words are not necessary. Being the chap he is though he says:

'Yes, but have you got these volumes?'

I'm beginning to tire of this.

'As I say, it is more a matter of what we can sell, and we are fully loaded on Churchill for now.'

There is a slight patrician tone to my voice now and he retreats a little, then comes back with:

'If I leave them with you and also the adventure stories, how much would you offer?'

I look at the pile of books.

'Around £6,' I say. I think this is too much really. I should still stick to the 30p rule for the Nevil Shute stories but maybe the Churchill volumes would merit the price.

'£7,' he says. Yes, he's definitely a pusher. But I want to close the deal. I look at him for a fraction of a second longer than he is comfortable with. Oh, to hell with it.

'Ok, £7.'

I punch the buttons on the till and give him the cash. The shop door tinkles. Kelvin appears. Useful. Useful. He looks at both of us curiously, his sixth sense scenting a sale going on.

'Kelvin. This gentleman has some possibly valuable aviation books which I have suggested he sell privately — would you perhaps like to verify that?'

I leave them to it and walk up to the Mind Body Spirit section where I need to do some sifting so as to stymie the existing chaos on its shelves. I can hear the ensuing talk though.

After a few moments and some keyboard tapping Kelvin says:

'What Anne told you is totally correct — your best bet is to take them home.'

– Yes!

'How much would you give me if I left them with you?' the chap says.

'£30,' says Kelvin without a second hesitation.

The chap is stunned.

'But you haven't checked them all,' he says.

'Don't have to,' says Kelvin 'that's my price.'

The two minds lock. I hum quietly to myself as I toss *The Essence of Calm* into the reject heap.

'Ok,' says the chap.

Incredible. If it was still dealing with me I would expect at least an attempt at a haggle. Post-feminism be damned. The unspoken power of a man in a suit is still alive and very very well. I hear the till open and shut. Deal done. Kelvin appears beside me.

'Right. I need to be elsewhere. So see you later.' He disappears.

The chap is still in the shop now browsing the mainstream fiction. I pass him carrying my load of discarded How-To-Do-Your-Life-Better books. I'm tempted to let fall the *Assertiveness or Aggression* book at his feet but instead say 'Well, that's all sorted then.'

He nods and says 'Don't worry, you'll get your money back, I'm going to buy some.'

I feel I am being treated a little like a petulant schoolgirl but reply 'Well, that's kind of you,' and carry on walking.

After fifteen minutes the chap appears at the till carrying a dozen books.

'Told you I would buy some,' he says. 'And I even bought one for my wife.'

'Good for you. At least you haven't forgotten her,' I say.

At this something seems to strike him.

'Maybe I should get her something else?' he swithers.

'Maybe,' I concur.

'What have you read?' he asks.

I suspect he is waiting for me to pick up something pink and glossy. I could do so but instead the thrawn and twisted part of me says 'You're probably asking the wrong woman. I've been around the literary world rather a long time. It could take me a bit of time to list everything.' Nasty. Snobbish. Yes I know. But there's only so much gender stereotyping I can take. I then relent. He did settle for a good price for his books. And he is now buying more. Maybe he enjoyed the haggling. I pick up a novel, *Hy Brasil* by Margaret Elphinstone.

'This. This is good. Perky intrigue. Decent research. Strong characters. Good plot. I really liked it.'

He takes me at my word and adds it to the pile. Pays. Puts his new books back in his bag and goes off whistling. Ach he was a nice chap really. I pick up the next Haynes manual and carry on.

The Panama Canal Effect

Every now and then a customer will throw us a random question which usually begins 'Em, 'scuse me, but do you have...'. It is, of course, not so random to them — it being the focus of their thoughts — but to us who have thousands of titles sloshing around inside our heads, the chance of being able to land information on the exact title requested and where it might be in the shop, can be a rather chancy affair. We are, however, occasionally helped by the intervention of the Divine — there is simply no other explanation for it. Co-incidence, accident, luck, are what others may call it, but these are just semantics for what can only be a miraculous helping hand. This belief is though a tad philosophical to explain to customers, so we have given it the shortened naming of 'The Panama Canal Effect' — a coinage founded by the following sketch. A sketch with a typical Kelvin twist.

Customer: Em ... I know this is long shot but I don't suppose you would have a book about the Panama Canal by McCullough ... published ...

Kelvin: (*Reaching into one of the boxes in the staff corridor*): This one?

Customer: (*Jaw dropping*) Yes! Exactly! That's amazing! You must really know your stock so well!

Kelvin: Well, we try to please.

Customer: How much is it?

Kelvin: It's a free item.

Customer: Sorry?

Kelvin: A free item — means you don't pay.

Customer: Don't pay? But ... (*looks around her*) ... isn't this a shop?

Kelvin: Yes, but we don't always ask customers to pay.

Customer: Um ... thank you ... (*still bemused*) ... but ... are you sure?

Kelvin: Absolutely.

Customer: (*putting book into her bag*). That's great! Good ... em ... right ... I'll ... eh ... well, I'll see you again.

She walks hesitatingly up to the door, turns around as if to say something, sees Kelvin calmly getting on with some work at the computer, decides against whatever she was going to say, pulls open the door, goes through, stops outside the window, stares in for a minute, shakes her head and walks off.

What this stunned but satisfied customer didn't know, and wasn't appraised of, was the fact that roughly nine minutes before she entered the shop I had been rummaging in History and had come across two copies of this book. It was one of those times where I was desperately trying to create space for twenty new-to-us books piled up on the table awaiting shelving. I was taking absolutely no nonsense from any books which appeared to be slackers — those which had sat around for far too long and hence appeared to be of no interest to customers. I had managed to jettison a bunch of books into the recycling boxes and McCullough's informative tome was one of them. I mean, who, just who, would want to read about the Panama Canal? And, if they did so desire, I had left one copy on its designated shelf. You may obviously wonder why then Kelvin didn't take the chance of making a sale, even if only £2.50. But, then again, being the intelligent reader you are, you have perhaps begun to appreciate that financial gain isn't always the desired outcome of an interaction with customers when Kelvin is involved. Opportunity for *outré* is quite often preferable to cold cash in his books. And I am quite sure that lady will return in company with at least one pal.

Maureece

I am standing on the elephant's foot so to reach up to the top shelves of Scottish Non-Fiction. Being rarely disturbed, the books up here enjoy a life of their own. They are mostly all slim but large volumes depicting Glasgow, Edinburgh, the Highlands, or the more interesting parts of Scotland in various manifestations. I think it true to say that I haven't yet witnessed any customer actually buying one of them. This may be because of their inaccessibility — we only have one safety step stool which may or may not be visible or known to the customer desirous of searching top shelves — or it may be that the books are either too dusty or simply uninteresting. Whatever the reason, I am determined to at least create some order up here — put Glasgow books with Glasgow books, Edinburgh with Edinburgh, (never the two together though … heaven forfend!), and weed out those who have sat here since the shop opened, and above all create some leverage. Customers are quite rightly wary of tackling any shelf at height which looks densely packed as one energetic tug could result in a rather dangerous landslide. And as we don't issue hard hats (although, now I think of it, that could be a novel and suitably quirky feature of the shop), it is best to make the stacking of shelves as safe as is possible. It is a job though which is not to be undertaken lightly, for as the female corpus of staff know all too well, sorting out top shelf books is itself a physical work-out and should only be done when feeling strong. As a road runner, the miles I walk in the shop each day doesn't cause much discomfort — indeed it's better to keep moving in the winter months when the woefully inadequate heating in the shop will chill static bones — but the exercise involved in reaching and lifting large books at a height are rather a challenge to my upper body strength. I am ploughing on with the task however, and gaining ground, when the shop door jangles. I look down and perceive a figure staring up at me.

I wonder at first if the sight is a result of blood rushing to my head from all the ascents and descents with large books that I have done in the last twenty minutes. I take a deep breath and hold on to edge of the bookshelf for a moment. I feel my pulse beating, yes a little fast, but nothing worrying considering what I have just been doing. So, the figure still staring at me is not a figment of blood pressure, but an entirely separate being. So separate in fact that I stare back for a full twelve seconds without blinking. The chap before me is distinctly kenspeckle. His drawn lined face is of indeterminate age but, if pressed, I would say he is certainly in the fifties-plus bracket. A lot of hard living has gone on in that skin previous to this date and his skeletal body is testament to it. He is clothed from head to foot in shades and textures of black slightly relieved by his flowing shoulder-length grey hair. On his head is the kind of felt hat — you know the type, yes you do — which d'Artagnan in *The Four Musketeers* would have worn and frequently doffed with a sweeping flourish. His body is encased in a long-sleeved tunic short coat, buttoned up to his protruding thin neck, his legs in what my younger brother once described as 'spray-on' leather trousers and calf-length Doc Martens. His left hand clenches a long black folded umbrella and from his right shoulder a black calf-skin satchel dangles. A faint musky smell, that makes me think of antique shops and auction rooms, fills my nostrils.

Some polite opening salutation is normal praxis in the shop. I unstick my tongue, blink my eyelids and say 'Good morning'.

'And good morning to you too, missy. To whom do I have the pleasure of speaking?' His voice is both cracked and strong with interesting inflexions of education.

I am about to reply when Kelvin's voice sails over the counter.

'Good grief! What are you doing here? It's still morning. Did you make a mistake?'

The man nods at me and sweeps past.

'No mistake. Oh no. I do not make mistakes. No. I run to the rhythm of my own drum. I also had to meet with a representative of the dentistry profession. But I do not wish to speak of that. No, I thought I would visit your literary emporium and enjoy the sweet delights of this hallowed place. How are you, sir?

'I'm very well, thank you, but what's that on your head?'

'This?'

The chap sweeps the wide hat off his head — with a swish worthy of Errol Flynn, waves it around a little then plops it back on his head. 'This is my hat, *mon chapeau*, for days when I need to do move at speed, disregarded by others and...'

'Disregarded? You'll probably find yourself on the front page of the local paper tomorrow.'

'Be that as it may. Fame is my fate. I wear it lightly. But tell me, who, whom is this female creature here?'

Kelvin scans round the shop trying to locate the person referred to.

'Which female person?'

'This one. This one in the truly amazing Alba-Gael plaid. This one who is fusing so beautifully with the books on our dear land.'

'Oh, have you not met yet? Yeh, she started work here a while ago.'

'Hallo there,' I say.

'This is Maurice,' Kelvin says.

'Hi Maurice,' I say.

'No. Mau*reece*. Mau*reece*. I am (flinging his arms out wide), Mau*reece*. Descendant of an auld alliance, a dalliance perchance, musician, artiste, troubadour, seeker of truth and good vibes.'

As the last word comes out of his mouth he drops his shoulder bag and brolly to the floor, adopts the pose of a base-guitarist and plays a riff on an air guitar.

'*Barrum. Barrum.*'

I get down off the step-stool with a couple of books. Somehow it seems safer to have my feet on the ground.

'And you, miss, or perhaps *Madame* Scotia,' our guitarist says 'are you a married woman?'

'Yes,' I answer. Madame Scotia?

'I respect that. I do. I respect that. He is a fortunate gentleman to be wedded to one of our true alluring Celtic women.'

'Um … thank you,' I say and deftly dodge around him to the staff corridor.

From the relative safety of this position — where I suddenly find it imperative to re-shuffle books awaiting sorting on a shelf — I can listen to Kelvin and Maurice blether. At least, it is a kind of blethering in that any simple question from Kelvin is met with a flow of words stemming from some kind of eclectic thought pattern in Maurice's brain. He has a wonderful way of running all that is passing through his mind into what comes out of his mouth. The famous literary exponents of the stream-of-consciousness technique — Proust, Richardson, Woolf, and Joyce

— could have learned from him. The eminent linguist, psychoanalyst and cultural theorist, Julia Kristeva, would view Maurice as a worthy illustration of her theory of 'the semiotic' as he so ably discharges pulsations of memory, narrative, sound and thought through his mouth and body.

'I said to that bitch in the bank … bitch … absolute bitch … in her smart suit and heels …'

'Eh, don't use that word in here please,' Kelvin cuts in.

'Bitch? You disprove of 'bitch'? No matter. No matter. If you object to my usage I will desist. Desist this instant. I respect your desire. Respect you as a man of wisdom and discernment. Why else would I come here? I pay hom*age*, hom*age* to this establishment. And now to Madame Scotia. This is my perfect scene. Here I am at ease. Ease with you both. I come to discuss, to …Walter Scott, that's the man … to *converse* with those worthy of conversing. The language of him! The language! And his affairs with the ladies. It is as I suspected. Lady Hamilton. *Mmmphm*. Yes. Hamilton. Now we all know. And I took those books from your shelf, creating neatness, order. It inspired me. I come here for inspiration. Rolling Stones have it man. *Barrummm Barrumm*. That's totally it man! Inspired.'

Kelvin is obviously used to this chap and simply ignores all the extraneous sounds. He seems unworried at the off-the-page behaviour of Maureece and calmly carries on checking book prices on the internet.

Having run out of jobs to do in the staff corridor I decide to be brave and head to the kitchen to put on the kettle. It's past 3.30pm. Kelvin will be reaching for the coffee pot. An inherited social etiquette in me prompts me to turn back and say to Maurice

'Would you like some coffee or a cup of tea?'

Perhaps this is unwise. Perhaps this chap is too unstable to offer refreshment to, but upbringing is upbringing, I cannot sit and drink tea in front of anyone without offering a cup to them.

'Coffee? No. No thank you. Coffee and me are not friends anymore. No. We are divorced forever. But tea. Yes. I will most gladly accept a cup of tea from *you*.'

Oh crumbs. Maybe this was a bad move.

'Ordinary or Green?' I ask.

'Green? What is this Green? Sounds exotic and enchanting. Like yourself Madame ...'

'It's supposed to be very good for you. I think it's a tea made from the very young leaves or something.'

'Ah, *virgin* tea. Yes. I will sample some of that.'

Still wondering about the wisdom of my offer, I make the tea and carry it back to the table.

'On the table,' I say.

'And I thank you,' he says galloping over and lifting the proffered cup to his mouth.

I have taken the precaution of putting some cold water in the hot brew — thus helping a quicker drinking time as otherwise I think we could be in for a long haul.

'*Mmmmm*. Delightful! This is truly delightful,' he murmurs.

Taking some more sips, he then places the cup back on the table and stares at me again. I smile and then look away.

'Have you, Madame, ever been filmed?'

'Whit?' I say.

'Filmed. On screen. Framed. Yes. Yes. I see it. I am a great judge of the photogenic. I know it instantly!' (He snaps his fingers.) 'Instantly! Yes. You will be in my film. It will be in Italia. It*aaaliaaah*. I will fly you out to the location in my private jet. You like to fly Madame?'

'Um…,' I falter. What is in his tea? I'm sure it is just hot water and normal Green Tea, no ginseng. Maybe it has still managed to rocket up a trigger-happy metabolism.

'Yes. I will fly on my plane to my house in It*aaaliaaah*. You must come. I will need you. You can be my muse.'

'Em. Thanks.'

'No, it is no *problema*. I will give you the best champagne. The best wine.' (Goes off into a torrent of pantomime Italian parlance …)

I leave my half-drunk cup of tea on the table. I think I should look busy.

'It will be *fantastique. Superbe. Bellisima.*'

He swallows the rest of his tea.

'But now, sadly, I must go. Goodbye Madame. *Bellissima. Bellisima.*'

'Ok. Bye. Nice to meet you.'

'And I am charmed to have met you. Charmed.'

As I walk past him en route to safer harbour of Scottish Non-Fiction, he reaches out and pulls me into a suffocating embrace.

Kelvin looks up from his coffee cup and says calmly 'Don't touch the staff, please.'

I disentangle myself and hot-foot it back to my step-stool.

Maurice bows to Kelvin's command, picks up his bag and brolly, sweeps an imaginary cape over his left shoulder. Salutes Kelvin. Doffs his hat at me and skims to the shop door. Pulling it open he fires back the final sally:

'See you in front of the cameras Madame Scotia.'

The shop door clangs. The bells batter together then fall silent.

'What ...' I say to Kelvin, '...what was that?'

'Just Maurice,' he says.

Maurice continues to delight us with his presence. At first he seemed to favour the afternoons and lingers on in the shop, filling our ears with hyper-babble, until, like storm-tossed shipwrecked souls we finally wash up onto closing time. But for the last few weeks he has taken to coming rather early in the morning — one day he was waiting outside for me to open up. I am now worried that he has built a visit to the bookshop into whatever weekly routine he has. It's not that he is not welcome in the shop, it's just that keeping one's mind on any task that requires thought or decision-making, is almost impossible. If we are busy with other customers when he arrives, he will usually occupy himself by perusing Art or Photography, taking a selection to the table where he will quietly sit, magnifying glass in hand, scanning their pages. When it becomes apparent to him that we are now free from other concerns, he will then move to the counter and begin his distinctive blend of verbal flow. If Kelvin is around he will take up the challenge thus allowing me to get on with other things. But, if caught on my own, I have to relinquish hopes of getting any thorough sorting done, find some basic kind of job and spend the next hour letting Maurice's view of life and the universe whirl around me. This is where it would just be so useful to be Sue Storm in the Fantastic Four — that force field of hers would be mighty handy for just these occasions. Unfortunately, lacking any such handy super power, I just nod and make monosyllabic noises in rejoinder to Maurice's gay repartee in the hope that he will eventually tire of the game and leave me in peace. I wonder sometimes how other members of staff cope. I notice that Lauren, our Saturday volunteer, retreats to the Sci-Fi, Crime and Horror vault, and works on as silently as possible. I can copy this strategy, if Kelvin is around, by tidying a shelf in the store room or giving the cludgie or kitchen a right good clean out, but other times I just try and avoid too much eye-contact and forge on with whatever I am supposed to be doing.

There are moments though when the urge to laugh out loud is huge. Such as when Kelvin happened to ask Maurice if he could have a pet, what pet would he have?

'Now, that's interesting,' answered Maurice striking the pose of Rodin's 'Thinker' (or, as Maurice would probably prefer me to call it, 'Le Penseur'). 'Only this morning as I was watering my cactus plants — my cacti, of the family cactaceae — and I thought how animal like they are. So ... yes ... I think I would have cacti and possibly a cheetah.'

'Fair enough,' says Kelvin. 'But how would the cheetah get on with our weather do you think?'

'Oh I would fly to my contact abroad and buy him the finest Afghan coat. Madame Scotia, I will also buy one for you.'

Oh help, he saw me smiling at his pet choice.

'Thanks, but I don't know if it is quite me.'

'Oh, but yes, yes! You have that rock n rolly Stevie Nicks thing going on sometimes. I notice these things. I notice. Yes, your sartorial dress intrigues me. Intrigues.'

Ah, time to disappear. The England section down the far corridor could surely do with a lengthy sorting out.

Then there was the time he told us he has been visited by Jehovah Witnesses. This was good.

'Yes, there they were. They asked if I believed in Jesus. So I, there and then, there and then I tell you, invited them in. I felt it was my duty to dispraise them of their religious bias. I am not against the concept of the Christ. No. No. But I really feel we can't have people running about talking unfounded rubbish. So I thought I had better help them to get their argument, their logic, their polemic, clear.'

'And did you?' says Kelvin his eyes lit up with the idea of the scene.

'I really feel I did. Yes. They said to me would I mind if they said hallo if they saw me in the street. I said by all means. By all means.'

Now that really must be a first. Maybe the Jehovah's are a lot more Christian than given credit for.

Maurice though proves the rule that it is fairly useless to categorise or label people as, once you know them a little more, there is always just that bit more to them. Maurice is a clever chap, he's intelligent, well read, he thinks deeply, is observant about life, he's courteous — sometimes in a rather cavalier medieval manner — but courteous he is. And there is a soulful nature hidden under his skin. I glisked this the time Kelvin asked him to give us a tune on his moothie. He whisked it out of a pocket and instead of some romping rocking bluegrass blast, played a gentle harmonious melody which made me think of wooden porches, rocking chairs, warm languid summer twilights, southern American accents, *To Kill A Mockingbird* and Miss Maudie's flowerbeds. Had various substances popular in the 60s not found their way into his veins — as is the rumour behind the man — I wonder what he would have done with his life — but would he have been the wonderful and incomparable character he is today?

Don't judge by the cover

The following scene occurred on one of the first occasions I happened to be in the shop on my own. My family and friends seem to like hearing it :

The shop door bells jangle violently as a tall, broadly built, young man explodes in. I move a little closer in behind the counter.

Me: Eh … Good morning…

(Apparent) Customer: Oh … hullo there.

Customer comes closer. Is sweating and out of breath.

Customer: I jist came in tae calm doon. Ye see, he went tae hit me. Ah cannae stand being touched. Ah know he's no right and it's no his fault. But he went tae punch me and ah couldnae help masel. Ah wis going tae swing fur him but then ah thought I should jist rin. So ah ran here.

Me: (*In a soothing tone as if speaking to a hot and tired child while silently feeling for my mobile phone in my pocket.*) Sounds like you did the right thing to move away. (But why here of all places? Why?)

Customer: Aye. Ah like this place. Helps me tae calm doon. Ye see ah jist couldnae take it. Ah jist couldnae. I still feel all angry.

Me: Upsetting.

Customer: Aye. Upsettin. Upsettin.

Me: Maybe you should just walk quietly home. (*Oh, please!*)

Customer: Naw. I'm here noo. I'll stay a wee bit. I'll go and look at the ancient Egyptian books. I like them.

Me: Very good. (Phew…The Egyptian shelves are a distance from the counter).

Door bursts open again. Two more young men appear both out of breath too. I wonder if there is a panic button underneath the counter.

Youngish man: Did a guy wi rid hair come in here?

As I hesitate to answer the other young man's voice comes sailing over the bookshelves.

'Aye, I'm here.'

'So ye ran away, Davy?'

I start to wonder if I should make my way to the front door. One of the young men comes towards the counter. Tattooed. Razor slash over one eye. I wildly run through my options …999 or landline call to local police station? Speed dial button on my mobile? Scream? Run for it? Skoosh him with the fly spray bottle under the counter? Or … wait. I wait.

Young man: 'Scuse me Missus. I wis jist wundering.

Me: Yes, sir? (If you want all the cash in the till … at this minute around £30 … you can have it. Have it.)

Young man: D' ye have any piano music?

Me: (*Trying to keep voice level*) Eh… yes. If you search in the box marked 'Piano' just up the corridor there, I think you'll find what you need there.

Young man, now legitimate customer: Right. Thanks Missus

He finds the box, drops to his knees and happily begins to rummage humming a quiet melody to himself.

Young man's pal: Davy ... are ye roon at the Egyptian bit?

'Aye. Ah'm here Mikey,' says a voice, now much calmer than when we were first acquainted.

Young man to me: He's aye on aboot thay Egyptians. Ye'd think there wis no ither folk in history. Ah keep tellin' him the Romans are mair interesting. But he disnae listen. Says they didnae dae much fur Scotland. But that's a pathetic argument. Ye hiv tae think global nae jist local.

Me: (*Sinking down onto chair behind counter*) Is that right?

Young man: Aye. There's some folk that are jist interested in whit happened on their ain front door step. That's pathetic too. Too narrow mindit. Too introspective. Onyway, hiv ye goat any books on Chaos Theory. Ah'm intae that at the moment. Interestin' stuff.

Me: The Science section down that corridor might have something on it for you.

Young man: Cheers. *Trots off whistling.*

I do a futile check under the counter. Kelvin, as already said, is fiercely teetotal, but I suspect that there could be many times in the days and months ahead of me that a hip flask, full of something stronger than tea, would be a welcome addition to the First Aid box. Must make a note in the diary to that effect.

The previous sketch was neatly followed up some weeks later when a thin white faced chap with an aura of hard street life came into the shop and pulled up smart at True Crime where he appeared intrigued. After some fifteen minutes perusal he wondered by the counter and said to Kelvin:

'Don't spose you've got any Shoppinhoor?'

'Shoppinhoor?' puzzled Kelvin. 'Eh, what does he write?'

'Philosophy an that,' the chap replied.

'Ah … yes sir. Schopenhauer. If we have any they'll be in Philosophy just up there on the right. Can't say though that I've seen anything by him of late.'

'Nae bother pal, I'll hiv a quick look.'

I ploughed my brain for anything on Schopenhauer. It comes back with a fuzzy memory of Florence Craye in Wodehouse — or was that Spinoza she liked? — and that highly intelligent aspergery young woman in the Dutch film *Antonia's Line*. Don't think deep study of old Schopenhauer did much for her quality of life. All that thinking about dissatisfied will would make anyone depressed and out of kilter with others.

'Think you're safer sticking with True Crime sir, I'm sure you want to enjoy your life,' I call to the chap.

He grins. Gets the joke.

'Aye. You're probably right.'

Never judge a book … Never judge a book …

Speak good. Yes?

The first time I encountered Marek was when his gangly form appeared before me and, by means of smiles and gestures, made me aware that he was keen to buy something on 'Scotteesh tartaaan, pleese'. It appeared though that the book he had had his eye on had been in the window, but now was not. Neither Kelvin nor I knew what had happened to it. We sell a few hundred books a week not to mention the latest wheeze of selling some stock on Amazon, so it is a bit difficult remembering what went where. Being nothing if not helpful however we proceeded to fire books of various shapes and sizes at Marek all pertaining to his chosen subject. Our rationale was that tartan *ergo* tartan does not change — unless you count the poncy designer stuff which every now and then tries to get taken seriously but actually gets no further than a catalogue picture. A Hunting Stewart, for example, has been that fusion of greens and yellows for a long long time — I speak with authority here as it was the tartan of my Primary School tie. And, as far as newcomers go, one of the most recent that made it into the established and recognisable tartan list was the infamous Black Watch, which, should you wish to know, will never be worn by anyone in sympathy with the 1715 Jacobite Rising as the regiment was set up to subdue the rebels and literally 'watch' the highlands. Marek however, being from Eastern Europe and very new to Scotland, had had little time to immerse himself in the intricacies of our history and persisted that the missing book was the only book which would correctly inform him of the whys and wherefores of Scottish tartan. He left the shop without said book but with the highly useful knowledge that the bookshop was stocked with people quite happy to follow his gestures and smiles and add words to his very limited knowledge of English.

Having promised we would do another search for his desired book, he returned the next day to hear of the results. The book had not surfaced and, as slight compensation, I offered him a cup of coffee. This offered the following veritable volley of social interchange:

Me: Would you like a cup of coffee? *Pointing at the coffee pot and making a gesture as if drinking.*

Marek: Yes.

Kelvin: No.

Marek: No?

Kelvin: Yes *please*.

Marek: Yes *pullease*.

Me: Milk? *Waving the wee cartons of the stuff so he would know what was being offered.*

Marek: Yes.

Kelvin: No.

Marek: No?

Kelvin: No *thank you*

Marek: No *theenk you*.

Kelvin: *Please* and *Thank you* are important.

Marek: Importantd? Importantd?

Kelvin: Yes. Important.

Just as I was wondering how in hell's name we could act out 'Important', Marek burrows in his bag and brings out what looks like a dictionary. Thank the gods for that. He gives it to Kelvin who looks up 'Important' with its consequent Czech Republic unpronounceable equivalent and points it out to Marek. Light dawns in Marek's face. He nods avidly. I wonder however if he gets that 'Please' and 'Thank you' are what we judge important — not the milk and sugar.

And on it went. We cycle through the 'Sugar?' sketch — I made the executive decision though to leave out the option of 'white or brown?' judging that it would all be just too much for Marek and for me. I doubt if the poor chap had every worked so hard for a cuppa in his life. When he finally got black coffee with three sugars he sank down at the table quite exhausted. Kelvin allowed him a few moments respite then took up his self-imposed role as teacher in rudimentary English.

Kelvin: What time is it?

Marek: Vot time ees it?

Kelvin: What time is it?

Me: *Pointing to wall clock.* What time is it?

Marek: *Looking at clock but making zero connection with it.* Vot time ees it?

Kelvin: What time?

I think this was the point I recognised that I just wasn't going to have the required energy or giftedness to continue this jog towards understanding, and quietly moved off to do something else.

Some fifteen minutes later Marek left the shop now armed with the knowledge that Scots may be keen on helping people buy books on their national dress, but were equally keen on knowing if you took milk and sugar and what the time was. Perplexing though this may have been for him, he nevertheless must have recognised that he had found a place where he could get a short burst of free tuition in basic English for the sum total of some mental sweat on his part.

Over the next few weeks Marek continued to pop into the shop ostensibly for his 'lesson' in the early afternoon, but perhaps too just for the simple human need of someone smiling, saying his name, offering him coffee and a few minutes of their time. Desirous though of learning English as quickly as possible Marek signed up for an ESOL college course. This was to begin in January and he was greatly looking forward to it. All his hopes of gaining employment in his new country rested, he believed, on how quickly he could learn English. One morning however I noticed him sitting on the wicker seat just inside the shop door. I say 'sitting' but Marek was more slumping 'like a half-filled sack' in the manner of Norman McCaig's disfigured dwarf in his poem 'Assisi'. We stumbled through some communication and it appeared that his longed-for college course was full up and he would not be able to begin the course until August which was some months later. Looking at his defeated spirit it seemed to me that all the past months of leaving his homeland — for whatever reason — travelling to a foreign land, finding a place to live, putting together all the necessities of day-to-day living, coping with the strange legal system and trying to make sense of the strange sounds the people emitted and expected you to understand, had finally hit him. All he could say was 'Ohgoost no good. Ohgoost no good'. I offered him coffee which he accepted — I didn't insist on the important 'Please and Thank you' niceties — and left him to his sad reverie.

Kelvin came in after a while and was appraised of Marek's news. One of Kelvin's bugbears is impotent bureaucracy. Realising how daft it was a for a beginner of English to attempt to wrestle out information from college administrators, Kelvin himself phoned the college to ask if the course was indeed full up and if so were there any others in the accessible area? I'm not sure of a definitive word for 'less than helpful' but, whatever it is, the college were most definitely it. Having raised Marek's hopes a little that someone with an extended vocabulary and a native knowledge could ascertain other available options for him, Kelvin also had to admit defeat. Marek slumped back in his chair. We carried on with bookshop things leaving Marek to ruminate about life's hardships.

Some time later the front door jangled and a chap came in. A local chap. One of our Rough-Harmless-But-Don't–Encourage-Too-Much customers. He made his way to the Crime vault just as Kelvin began to speak to Marek. The chap was interested in the interchange. Kelvin explained that Marek was new to our country and needed to learn English.

'Sat right ma man,' says the chap. 'Weel, ah kin help ye there.'

At that he sits himself down at the table and carries on.

'Right. Let's dae yer numbers. Ye always need the numbers. Right aifter me pal. Say 'Waaan, twooo, threeee, foourrr ...'

Marek gets what's happening. Brightens a little.

'Waaan? One?'

'Aye, that's it pal. 'Wan' is Scottish. Mair useful fur ye if ye want tae live here. But ye kin always say 'One' if ye want. Right c'mon. Twoo, threeee, foourrrr, ah we're daein great.'

And they went on counting up to 'Fufty'. Then the days of the week, then the months of the year. Marek had got his wish. If he couldn't go to a class the gods had organised a class to come to him. Strange how things work out.

The old adage however that one should always be careful of what one wished for, came into effect towards the end of the 'lesson'. Marek had dashed out of the shop to get his dictionary which he had left at home so he could explain something to his new teacher — who was now happily slurping a cup of coffee and no doubt congratulating himself on a good job done. I passed the table saying:

'It's kind of you to talk to Marek. He was really down this morning as he couldn't get on an English class.'

'Nae bother,' says the chap. 'Ah'm gonnae tell him when he gits back that me and ma mates kin aw bundle intae his place and we'll ah teach him. Nae bother. Nae bother at a.'

I made a mental note to warn Marek to be rather evasive about his address and hoped his dictionary would have the word listed, otherwise we were in for a long and complicated pantomime which would leave him thinking that Scottish people were keen on slippery words that don't really mean what they say. And that would just be taking acquisition of his new language to a shudderingly complicated level.

Biblical lather

'Hallo there,' says a voice.

I look up from the pile of the ever popular Jacqueline Wilson books I am cleaning and pricing. I recognise him as an infrequent yet somehow significant customer. But who exactly? My brain starts scanning the possibilities. Largish chap, bumbly type, wearing a Conan Doyle rat-catcher hat, a check shirt, corduroy breeks, tweed tie, much used and loved wax jacket and holding a battered leather briefcase. Old school. Ah, yes, Bible Man.

'Do you remember me?' he asks.

I quickly flip my labelling of him into the more polite 'Bibles. You're interested in bibles.'

'Yes,' he says, pleased I remember, 'but only the Authorised version.'

I want to quip back 'Are there unauthorised versions — has Posh come up with one?' but a quiet little alarm is beeping persistently inside my head — one needs to be caw canny with customers keenly interested in bibles, there is always a good chance any slight interest shown beyond editions and printing history will slip into a major treatise of faith practices and belief systems. And that's dodgy ground. So I simply go down the staff corridor and look where Kelvin tends to leave any bibles.

'There don't appear to be any,' I call to him.

He obviously doesn't believe me.

'Can I come and look?' he says starting down the corridor.

'Em, no, sorry, shop policy,' I say.

What is it about second-hand bookshops that people think they can stravaig into parts clearly marked 'Private. Staff Only'? I presume it is because they think that we are either deliberately hiding the book of great price or aren't capable of recognising it. Anyway, he respects my refusal to have him mooching about the shelves and then asks:

'And, do you have a gents' toilet here? Can I use it?'

This is another problematic question.

'Again, no, not for customers, we don't.'

I think about echoing Kelvin's reasoning that you wouldn't ask to use the staff toilet in a shoe shop. I momentarily ponder on explaining the whole Health and Safety issue of having customers wade through the busy back store and the obvious hygiene concerns of cleaning the cludgie. But that feels pointless and instead I direct him to a nearby pub who seem to be ok with people using their loo. They probably hate us doing that but it's what I have been told to do and at least I feel I am helping the desperate customer. He trots off, quickly, over the traffic lights. I carry on with Jacqueline Wilson.

Four minutes later he's back looking more relieved. Problem now is that he's ready for a good chat. He begins with a run through of who was in the shop last time he was here. He wants to know who is who. I tell him and as I do so notice that there's something a bit weird with his eyes. They are distinctly bulbous and seem to blink only every two minutes and that's done with the rapidity of a darting fly. The subject of staffing was only the preliminary warm up and he swings into the subject of bookshops. We bemoan the demise of Borders in Glasgow — we both agree that it was always busy, was a good place to meet and that we miss it. He then asks if he can have some coffee.

Of course,' I say although my heart sinks. This means another good twenty minutes or so. We talk about coffee a bit and why our shop gets this particular brand. Mundane subjects now done, he then turns back to the theme of bookshops and what follows is rather confusing.

'Have you been into Arouet and Jean-Jacques lately?' he enquires.

'No, not for a while. I did hear though that the lane is threatened with closure.'

'Really? Oh dear. That's terrible. But now I don't know this Elaine. I thought the bookshop was run by two brothers. Does she also own that bookshop on Great Western Road?'

'Alba Books?'

'Yes, that's the one. So she owns that too does she? Well I didn't know that.'

'Em, no, I didn't mean...'

'Well, that's good to own a few shops.'

I should leap in again and correct the misunderstanding. But, what the heck, it's more fun this way. He then offers the opening line of his pièce-de-résistance:

'And what about those zombies in America?'

'Sorry ... what?'

'Zombies. Yes, apparently people are taking soap suds — soap suds of all things — and it sends them mad. Do you not know about the case last week?'

'Er, no, I hadn't heard.'

Oh, dear. Zombies. And him with his staring bulbous eyes.

'Yes, this woman took this stuff and it sent her mad. She tried to strangle her dog then tried to chew the face off her two sons — didn't manage it though — and then took off all her clothes and rushed out into the street. The police came for her and asked her to come peacefully. Well, she didn't of course. So they had to stun her and that didn't work so they had to lasso her and pin her to the ground and they got her that way.'

'Aye, in your dreams, boys,' is what I want to say. But I don't because I am holding onto my lips and my sanity. He stands around two feet away from me totally intent on his story, his eyes now three times as large and he hasn't blinked for a long while. Bibles and zombies. Oh dear Lord. I can feel my lips twitching. I need to say something before I start giggling.

'Yes, well counter-balancing that terrible stuff are all the good things happening in the world.'

Bland. Evasive. Not excellent badinage but it'll have to do. I need to break him out of whatever trip he's on.

'Oh, of course. Of course,' he says clearly a little crest-fallen that I'm not writhing in the gore of the story.

Then something seems to click back into place behind his eyes. He harrumphs a bit then puts his now empty cup down. Lifts up his briefcase and says:

'So, regards to all. Best be on my way,' and shambles his way out of the shop.

What, just what was in that coffee? We diligently wash out the thermos flask after close-up every day. But maybe I should have a sniff for any lurking soap suds.

The Learned Will Shine

There are countless comical sketches happening in the shop which provide huge entertainment but leave us unchanged in thought or outlook — apart from wondering if it really is us who are mad. There is however another side to the story which would be easy to go unmarked and dismissed. Whenever the owner is quizzed as to why he wanted to open a bookshop when he had already had an academic career and was in a position to retire without financial worry, he tends to say that he needed something to do and this is no more than a hobby which gets him out of the house. A measure of this is true. However, if you consider Kelvin's policy of tolerance of and interest in those often viewed as out of kilter with mainstream society, and his patience with those whose highlight of the day is to come to the shop, be given a cup of coffee and enjoy airing their views on life, with the occasional buying of a book, Cloisters is far more than a straight-forward commercial enterprise. As Kelvin remarked recently 'We seem to be part bookshop and part drop-in centre'. Some of the drop-ins are complicated as they demand and feed on our attention, want to sit at the table for an hour or more, don't want to peruse the shelves unaccompanied and haven't yet grasped that good conversation requires the allowance of reply and is not styled as a monologue. The uncomplicated are those who are grateful for a hot cuppa, are interested in the books, offer in exchange good conversation and never outstay their welcome. I have to say the balance does sometimes tend to tip towards the former type and I come home feeling as if I have just spent seven hours in a day care centre.

The bookshop however does also function as a bookshop. And for many people the fact of its existence is a joy and sheer delight. The curious mix of the esoteric, the eclectic and erudite fills them with something of the same excitement that one might feel on discovering an old attic filled with forgotten treasures. As I have already declared, Cloisters is a place of difference. A place to pause and peruse in. And if the staff aren't too busy dealing with a problematic person, is also a place to ask advice on reading that will answer and advance a seeking spirit. These are the customers who remind me why I might be in the right place, for there is nothing I enjoy so much as the question "Can you suggest any decent authors who write about...." So thus it was how I met Michael.

It's hard to remember exactly when Michael first came into the bookshop. He wasn't a regular, more of a every-now-and-then kind of customer. And, thinking of it, his visits probably coincided with when he had given himself space for play. It would make sense then that he came in during some school holiday period as he was, I have since heard, unrelenting in the pursuit of his studies. Extended reading outside of his school syllabus was, I imagine, kept for times of leisure. Where other schoolboys might chuck their scuffed books into the darkest corner of their rooms and with a sigh of contentment log on to Facebook or an interrupted electronic game, Michael revelled in the opportunity for reading and the visiting of bookshops. But then, they said he was always different from the crowd. And this was patently obvious when one first encountered him.

There are not many seventeen year old lads who would choose to wear a silk cravat, shirt, tailored jacket, skinny plum-coloured jeans and pointed shoes as 'hang-out' gear. And while shoulder-length hair is once more 'in' for lads, even had it not been, I suspect Michael would have grown his to that length just for aesthetic effect. 'Raffish' is, I judge, the word that best described his dress-sense and, in the West of

Scotland, that look is rather rare. He wore his clothes with an unaffected determination as if he knew he was dressing differently but it was what he liked.

It was however, more his question to me about authors that were 'a bit like Oscar Wilde' that caught my attention. Normally, if seventeen year old lads came in the shop at all they made a bee line for our graphic comics box — Judge Dredd and the like — or went straight to the Sci-Fi shelves. Sometimes they would immediately ask for some canonical title — recognisable as required reading for Higher English — look at its length, sigh, buy it and leave the shop. On other occasions I would suggest to a desperate parent about to embark on a holiday with a reluctant teenage son, that Tony Hawks' *Round Ireland with a Fridge* or Mark Haddon's *The Curious Incident of the Dog in the Night* were usually sure fire hits if their offspring wasn't into Sci Fi ,Vamp Lit, Graph Com, Sport and felt too old to be seen reading *Harry Potter* or any of the Anthony Horowitz series. Another good one is Dodi Smith, (she of *101 Dalmatians* fame), and her nostalgic novel *I Capture the Castle* (c. 1940s) which I have given as a gift to many a teenage lass. It is stuck in my head as more suitable for girls — although disproving that theory is the fact that my son read it at the age of seventeen but as he was at that point in life smitten by a first love who was 'into reading', there may have been some underlying impetus there. I wonder though that I didn't mention it to Michael as, the more we talked, I comprehended what he liked were stories with quintessential English settings with the optional extra of a touch of farce. Instead of Smith I suggested PG Wodehouse. To my surprise Michael hadn't read him. As we didn't have any in our second-hand fiction section I showed him a smart paperback series published by Arrow Books, an imprint of Random House, in our 'New but Cheap' shelves. I left him to read the blurb on the back of some of them and went back to whatever it was I had been doing. Five minutes later I heard him discussing with his friend — or cousin as it turned out to be —how many they could carry.

'You don't want them all?' I asked.

'Eh, yeh, they look good,' he replied.

'But what if they don't measure up to your expectations?' I persisted 'It would be a bit of an expense.'

'No, I will like them. I know I will,' he equally persisted.

I was about to say 'fair enough' and go and look for a box to put the books in when his cousin, whom I later learned was called Christopher, said he wasn't going to carry them and anyway he thought it would be stupid to take the whole series when Michael hadn't read any.

Michael demurred a little but I could see he was still keen. We do sometimes find that customers are attracted to the notion of owning a set of books, but I was a little worried that he might not find them to his taste. A customer had recently said he thought Wodehouse was 'upper-class pretentious rubbish out of touch with all that was going on in the world' — to which I replied 'but you have to admit his use of superlative is second to none' (I was quoting but didn't admit to it). I don't recall the customer's answer.

Anyway, the upshot of the wrangle with his cousin was that Michael decided to take three volumes and come back in for more. And they left merrily punching each other with their bags.

And come back he did about a fortnight later. This time my husband was in the shop, Kelvin either having gone home early or was having a day off. It was around half past three — the customary tea break time for staff. As coffee is not my usual tipple, especially the bookshop coffee as it is stalwart stuff and not for the faint of heart, I put the kettle on in the kitchen to make tea. When I returned I found Michael in the shop, along with the same lad and a woman.

'Ah, Mr Wodehouse,' I sallied, 'How goes life?'

'Yeh, good,' he grinned. 'I really like those books, and I want some more, but are there any other authors you think are any good that write about that time?'

Ah, I sensed a personal *belle époque* emerging.

Just as I was about to suggest something by the contemporary writer Alan Hollinghurst — our book group having just read A *Stranger's Child* — my husband came in with:

'*Brideshead* … yes, *Brideshead* … I think you'll like him. He's round here.'

And off they went to our Classics section (or what Kelvin stubbornly terms 'Literature' — a coinage which would keep literary theorists debating for decades).

Leaving Michael in capable hands I went back to the kettle, made a pot of tea and returned to the main bookshop carrying the teapot and some cups. The woman who was with the two lads had sat down at the table to wait for them. I asked her if she would like some tea and seeing that I was going to sit down too, she accepted. While my other half strolled with Michael around the shop talking of Waugh's text and then other of his favourites such as Gerald Durrell and John le Carré, I chatted with the woman who turned out to be Michael's mum, Terry.

I said to Terry that I was impressed with the span of Michael's literary interests. She was obviously both used to this — having no doubt heard it numerous times from his teachers — but still proudly told me of how Michael, had passed the entrance exam and had been interviewed (without tutoring, as is apparently usual), for a place at Oxford to read Politics, Philosophy and Economics. Out of the 3,000 hopeful candidates contesting for the precious six places, Michael made it through to the last 38. One of the candidates was a twenty-four year old Chinese man who was the world debating champion — such was the calibre that the sixteen year old Michael stood his ground with. Terry said that when Michael had first told her he was applying she had replied something to the effect that Oxford wasn't for the likes of young people educated at a west of Scotland state school. 'Watch this space,' had been Michael's reply. So, although not finally gaining a place in the dreaming spires and hallowed colleges of Oxford, Michael had had great fun during his trip there — taking an open air bus around its archetypal streets and ancient buildings; rummaging in the book and charity shops; having a drink in the various pubs which the likes of Charles Dickens' son and CS Lewis and JRR Tolkien had frequented; charming his way into exclusive college halls; delighting in and soaking up the atmosphere of deep history, culture and scholarship. Michael had already been accepted to study at St. Andrew's University — one of Scotland oldest and finest universities — and was looking forward to matriculating in the autumn. His game plan now was to complete his undergraduate degree in St Andrew's and then apply for a Masters in Oxford, believing that by then he would be more than ready for any interview. Terry's eyes sparkled as she spoke of how proud she was of her lad particularly as neither she nor Michael's dad came from an academic background.

'Well, judging by the reading he's already doing,' I said 'he'll be way ahead of many other students.'

We talked a bit more and, once the others had finished circumnavigating the aisles, they joined us at the table. I had then to deal with some other customers but my husband and Michael enjoyed a high old chat about books.

A half hour later Michael, with his mum and cousin, trotted off content with a paperback copy of Waugh's *magnus opus* tucked under his arm. Yes, the doings of Lord Sebastian, his teddy Aloysius, all that high class Oxbridge stuff and musings on the divine operation of grace, would be entertaining stuff for this lad who had his heart set on higher things.

It was then quite some time until I saw his aunt in the shop along with Michael's cousin. They were in search of a copy of *Macbeth* which we found easily enough and, having recognised the young lad as Michael's cousin, asked how Michael was doing at university. The aunt dropped her shoulders, sighed and then told me that Michael hadn't been able to take up his place. What was initially thought to be a simple pulled muscle in his leg —a sports injury even though Michael never played sports — turned out to be something much much more serious. Michael was undergoing intense chemotherapy as we spoke. Despite this very unexpected turn of events she spoke very positively about the prognosis and said that Michael had appeared to accept what had happened and was determined not to let it alter his enjoyment of life. Apparently, when he had had his first round of chemo for the day, he was signing out of the hospital and going off down the west end of Glasgow and having a fun time in the cafes, bookshops and charity shops before returning for his second treatment. He was also loving all the time he now had for reading and watching his favourite films.

'That's bravely done,' I said

'He's like that. Always has been. Determined to do his own thing. That's what's keeping him going now,' replied his aunt.

'Tell him to come and see us if he can,' I said, wondering if that would be possible.

True to form Michael did visit. Devoid of his lovely golden locks but in company with his mum, two of his aunts and his same bright impish grin. And in line with the six degrees of separation theory, one of the aunts was none other than the wonderful Grace who was the childminder of my son many years ago and earth mother to most of our old neighbourhood. Grace told me that Michael had spoken of the bookshop and how much he had enjoyed his bookish blether with 'the long-haired owner' — it hadn't occurred to my husband to make it clear that he didn't actually work there but just hung out in the shop every so often. We had a laugh at that and then dived into catching up on all the news of our respective offspring and had a cheery time of it. While we women talked about who had gone on to study what, who was working where and who had married who, Michael swarmed over the shelves, interested as ever in books.

Having made the connection with Grace I remembered that she belonged to a large family of sisters which was why I was having trouble working out names to very similar faces. I still hadn't quite got the grasp of this when another aunt of Michael came into the shop some weeks later — a sister who was so like Grace that I began speaking to her without realising it was a totally different person. Fortunately this wasn't unusual for her and she laughingly explained who she was. She then told me of Michael and that the news wasn't good. The cancer had spread to his lungs, the tumour in his leg had enlarged and he was scheduled to undergo a major operation. The most horrible thing for his parents was that the surgeon had said that if the tumour could not be removed safely they might have to amputate his leg — to which, Michael had apparently rejoined 'What need have I of legs with a brain like mine?' A riposte apparently typical of Michael who was also reportedly enjoying pestering the oncology medical staff to give him a full elucidation of his condition.

Michael's operation was scheduled for mid January — one week after his 18th birthday celebration. It was currently coming up for Christmas. As the bookshop got busier with people buying unusual books for gifts and ordering book tokens for people who would prefer the fun of rooting out titles for themselves, I thought of Michael. I wondered how it went with him and what must he be feeling. For all his bravado and refusal to be brought low by the cruelties of cancer, he must, I knew, have times of fear and doubt. I thought of *The Way of the Peaceful Warrior* by Dan Millman. In this book a young promising gymnast sustains a serious injury which puts paid to his hopes of becoming a world class athlete. He happens upon an older man working as a garage attendant who is much more than he seems. Through a series of events the young man realises that the older one has much to teach him and that sickness and doubt in mind and body are but paths to deeper learning, if we pay attention to them. It is a powerful book and somehow has achieved the right balance of spiritual teaching and accessibility without being the stuff of fluff and fairytales. I pondered on getting a copy for Michael. Then wondered if this would seem arrogant. Who was I to say to a young lad facing a deeply worrying operation that there was something to be learned by it? I decided instead that if Michael came through the operation I would source a copy of Millman's book and then give it to him. In the meantime, in my need to do something for him, I bought a classy Paisley-patterned hardback notebook with a pen, wrapped it up with a card and took it to his aunt's house — I had no idea where Michael lived but knew that Grace could be trusted to pass it on. There have been times in my own life when I have been dealt a difficult hand and have found that to write out my rage, hurt or frustration is cathartic. Perhaps it would be so with Michael. At the very least he would know he was not forgotten by the bookshop folk.

Christmas came and went. January progressed. I knew Michael's operation was to be sometime mid January but couldn't recall the date. I was busy with my own life — my family, my friends, my home, my paid job, my writing projects, my piano lessons, my road running, my dogs, my book club, and a myriad of other minutiae that fill my days. Time slipped by. Then, one day towards the very end of January I came home to find the answer machine light flashing. I pressed the button to hear Grace's voice telling me that Michael had died a few days previously.

The rain was drizzling down outside and I had been glad to get home, but my response to Grace's news was to call the least problematic one of my dogs, slip on her lead and head back outside for a walk. My head needed time to sift the impact of the news. I needed the hush and solitariness that a stroll in the late afternoon winter rain can give. As I came out of the front door I noticed a slate had worked itself loose from the roof and smashed into shards on the path. Somehow the image was in tune with the news of Michael's passing.

I called Grace that evening and heard all that had happened. Amidst all the detail of the operation, the complications, the rising and falling hopes, she also told me how the whole extended family had got together the week before the operation to celebrate Michael's 18th birthday, the fun they had had, the photographs they had taken. If a family could have done more to support an ailing lad, I doubt they exist. She also said that Michael's mum had specifically asked that I was told of Michael's death as the bookshop had been one of his most favourite places. Just before she put the phone down Grace said with a breaking voice 'Thank you for being kind to Michael'. I couldn't answer.

Two days later my husband and I went to the Requiem Mass for Michael. In some ways I wasn't quite sure why I was going. I wasn't a close friend of the family or of Michael. Indeed I wasn't Michael's friend at all, just 'the woman in the bookshop', but there was some need in me to go and I think it was because I felt I understood Michael's mindset — his thirst for writing that would teach him something and continue to do so, his enjoyment of the aesthetic, the classical, the academic. Had he lived I would have watched his career with interest and would have been surprised had he not found a home in academia teaching either philosophy or literature. It is a world I understand and my heart was heavy that we would never have bantering chats about the quirks of literary theory or the strange premise of a philosophical stance.

The church was a large one but every seat was taken. The crowds were both a testament to Michael and to people's utter dismay that such a gifted lad had been taken from them. On the front cover of the specially designed booklet was a photograph of Michael — healthy and happy, flowing curls billowing, cravat carefully tied, amused smile well in place. For those members of his family who last saw him battered by chemotherapy, steroids, drugs and surgery it will take some time for the more beautiful images of him to return. But having last met him as he really was — young, aspiring, full of life and originality — my image of him had not been damaged. There were many words spoken of Michael at his Requiem, all of them telling of his uniqueness, his giftedness, his intelligence and his way of living life without compromise. There were funny stories where the congregation laughed, there were sentiments and memories which caused tears to blur our eyes. The first reading was a careful extract taken from the prophet Daniel, chapter 12:

> At that time Michael will stand up, the great prince who mounts guard over your people. [...] When that time comes, your own people will be spared, all those whose names are found written in the Book. [...] The learned will shine as brightly as the vault of heaven, and those who have instructed many in virtue, as bright as stars for all eternity.

It was in so many ways appropriate for Michael. Not only the obvious mention of his own name, but the fact that Michael's favourite song of late had apparently been 'I'm Still Standing' by Elton John and the fact that Michael was drawn to deep scholarly learning. Well chosen indeed. The celebrant urged the congregation to look to Michael's example and be interested in learning, in books, no matter our circumstances or usual habits. Michael's teacher, who had taught him Higher English, gave her own personal tribute to her former pupil and all that he had been to her. She told us of how Michael had given her fair copies of essays submitted to her once all the exams were over, how he had left quotations by

Dickens on her doorstep, how he had emailed her Horace Mann's line 'Be ashamed to die until you have won some victory for humanity,' some months before he died as he was excited that his sarcoma was to be sent to a specialist research unit in Oxford, how he had moved from being a rather intimidating pupil to a valued young friend and how much she would miss him.

> His shrewd and witty observations about fellow pupils, staff and organisation of the school system generally were refreshing and made me laugh on the most thankless of school days. Michael hated conformity, platitudes and blandness; he saw through hypocrisy and pomposity and pointless bureaucracy and undercut it mercilessly with his lacerating wit.

> He was an original in a world of replicas. When others in his English class embraced the chance to use the Show-Me Boards, Michael would just raise his eyes incredulously at the very idea that he would use an item whose name was also an instruction on how to use it, and whip out his fountain pen and pad of paper in defiance.

Protégées like Michael are a rare find for any teacher and the loss of one so talented is a cruel cut.

When we came of out the church into the bitter January day, most people made for their cars so to be ready to form part of the cortège that would make its way to the crematorium where they would say their final good-bye to Michael. I stood watching the huge cavalcade move off and saw that the local police had come to stop all other traffic to let Michael and his mourners through.

Later that day in the quiet of my house, I sat down to write to his parents. Much had been said of Michael but I had my own message to give. On sheets of handcrafted paper — for what else would suffice for such a young man? — I told them of how the Greeks had a belief that when someone died while still in the first flush of adulthood, it was deemed as the noblest way because the body and spirit of that person would never know the decay and confusion of old age. 'It is of little comfort to you,' I wrote, 'but your son will remain thus perfect in the minds of us blessed to have known him.'

Some days later, reaching into a box of books that had come into the bookshop, my hand touched upon something soft. My fingers fastened around it and I pulled out a small purple suede-bound 1911 volume of Oscar Wilde's poetry. Its edges were scuffed, its corners turned up, its end-papers stained with the passage of time, its gilt lettering on the front cover dulled, its printed pages foxed and faded. It had been carried in a coat pocket, a jacket pocket, a shirt pocket, a trouser pocket for many years. It had been read over and over again. It had been cherished. I turned it over in my hands and thought of Michael.

Epilogos

Many months after Michael's death I met with Terry. I had sent her my chapter on Michael and had asked if she would read it over, correct anything that needed correcting, and, most importantly, give me permission to publish. I wasn't sure if the family would want the story of their precious lad to be in print, I wasn't sure if I was trespassing on sacred ground — were my words good enough to honour their special lad? Bolstering up my courage I reminded myself of what I used to say to undergraduate students in my care. Students who had opted for an Arts degree, students who wanted to read and know of literary things instead of a more muscular scientific or technological field of study. The young men in particular would sometimes tell me of how their mates thought their decision to focus on literature and language was of no practical use, was a little namby-pamby, artsy-fartsy and whatever.

'Wait,' I would say, 'Your skill, and it is a skill, as a wordsmith is needed. There will be occasions in life where words will offer something of vital substance, of durability, of lasting value, which other fields of study cannot offer.'

As I drove towards my meeting with Terry I prayed that my own advice would prove true.

Terry had already spoken briefly with me on the phone. She and her family had read my piece on Michael and were happy for me to go ahead and publish, but there was more she wanted to tell me. More about Michael that demonstrated just how incredible a young man he was.

I meet with her in a cafe of a nearby park one beautiful September afternoon. We sat outside in the surprisingly warm sunshine both us enjoying the air, the sound of people and birds at play and Sunday ease. Terry spilled photographs of Michael onto the table. Far from me worrying if I would be prying into her memories of her son, she was eager to talk about and give detail of the extraordinary spirit that was Michael.

Some of the photos were of Michael's interview week in Oxford. Others were of him at various parties. In line with his determined sense of fashion, Michael got great fun out of dressing up in various guises whenever the occasion demanded. There were photos of him as Jay Gatsby from Fitzgerald's classic novel, as the grotesque Joker in the nurse's uniform from *Batman*, and as Cardinal Wolsey — Lord Chancellor to Henry VIII of England. How, I wondered, did Michael know of Cardinal Wolsey? Was it that he had perhaps studied Robert Bolt's play *a Man for All Seasons* which focuses on St Thomas More, the successor to Wolsey? Or was it — as I learned, after consulting Peter Ackroyd's biography of More which I found in the bookshop a few days later — the fact that Wolsey had a love of display and rather outrageous style? I smiled to myself at Michael's choice of disguise. Where his contemporaries would probably opt for throwing a bed sheet over themselves and making ghostly noises, or come dressed as a dice, Michael favoured the slightly esoteric, the elegant, the mysterious. It made sense then when Terry told me that Michael had been a member of the Magic Circle — the premier organisation for magicians — and had loved performing magic tricks from a young age. Ah, the lure of illusion, of carnival, of suspension of the usual. I was beginning to get it. It fitted too when Terry went on to tell how Michael had stunned the punters waiting in a chip shop in a socially challenged area of Glasgow one evening, by boldly strolling in wearing a long purple velvet coat and gloves and carrying a stylish walking cane.

'Are they … are they wummin's gloves?' one of the goggle-eyed customers had asked.

'Perhaps,' answered Michael, coolly sweeping past.

It was in further accord then, when Terry handed me a copy of Michael's dissertation for his Advanced Higher English, to see that it was a comparative study of the literary doppelgänger as constructed in *The Picture of Dorian Gray* by Oscar Wilde, *The Strange Case of Dr Jekyll and Mr Hyde* by Robert Louis Stevenson and *The Private Memoirs and Confessions of a Justified Sinner* by James Hogg. All novels which lingeringly pivot on the question of doubleness, of dark and troubled parts of the psyche. These are titles not out of place on undergraduate courses and, when I found time to read Michael's dissertation some days later, discovered that his writing would not be out of place in a pile of second year undergraduate essays either. What saddened me though was that I could see where Michael's poised and already mature critique of literature, would have been sharpened and developed at university. All the potential for a first class honours degree was already there in his writing. All he needed was immersion in academic thought, good supervision and time. And it was time that was denied him.

But Michael lived his life to the last moment. Terry repeated to me how Michael, the day before his massive operation, had astounded the worried hospital staff by signing out and going, with his cousin Charles, to see the film version of *Les Miserables* which was being screened in the city centre. I thought how good it was that he had seized his day and did what his heart had told him to do.

After an hour or so of listening to Terry speak of her son she suddenly asked, with quiet desperation in her voice:

'Do you think there is life after death? What do you think of all that?'

Is there a mother on earth, who has lost her child, who doesn't want to be assured that there is something else, something more to come? But, as Hamlet soliloquised, it is but 'an undiscovered country, from whose bourn / No traveller returns', and all I could offer were my own faltering thoughts:

'There must be something. Otherwise, where does love go?' I said. 'Where does the essence of each of us, that is nothing to do with the material body, where does that go? I don't know what form the next existence takes but I believe there must be something that is as yet beyond our ken. A biblical passage tells us that 'the eye has not seen, nor the ear heard, the things that God has prepared.' That's what I hold on to.'

It wasn't much but, perhaps just in the asking of the question, it lanced a little of her overburdened heart. And I felt privileged to have been asked.

Terry also shared how that she had often wondered if Michael knew how ill he was and that he had never voiced any fears to her. She had asked the surgeon about this when she made a return visit to the hospital shortly after Michael had died.

'Oh that lad knew all right,' said the surgeon 'there was little that got past him.'

While he was ill Michael had received a book of Housman's poems from another teacher who also became a friend. He texted her back his favourite among them — a short two verse extract from 'A Shropshire Lad' which begins 'Into my heart an air that kills' — a poem usually understood as a nostalgic look at a past which cannot be repeated, but it was perhaps Michael's admission that he knew exactly what was happening to him even if he was loathe to dwell on or speak of it. It seems that along with his cleverness and his deliberate provocative wearing of a T shirt which proclaimed 'I will be nicer if you try to be smarter,' was a profound care for and protection of those in his inner circle whom he loved.

Terry also reiterated how Michael encouraged people to aim for excellence in whatever they did. When his girlfriend, Rachel, decided to study Law he told her not to mess about in applying for jobs in any old tin-pot firm but to go for one 'with a big fountain and all that'. Uncannily enough, some time after Michael had passed away, Rachel did successfully apply to a firm which she discovered, on walking into the foyer, boasted a beautiful fountain. Michael, it seems, is still weaving magic.

As a friend, who started out as a tutor but who quickly gave up that title on realising the extent of Michael's literary knowledge, wrote after Michael's death:

> As I write this, I imagine him organising literature classes for saints, and what an honour that would be to belong to that heavenly class, where I feel confident he will be re-writing the Bible in Bob Dylan style, with a backing group of Angels singing 'The Times They Are A-Changing.' I would even risk a fiver that before long people will start to notice an addition to the traditional Bible — maybe something along the lines of 'Michael's Letter to the Citizens'. [And] I have taken your advice Michael, and am reading more of the poetry of Philip Larkin ...

So on days when the bookshop chills my bones because of the inadequate heating, or days when there are too many daft folk making demands, or days when people are dischuffed when we refuse to buy their water-damaged and smoke-ridden books, or when I worry a little over the safety aspect of the shop, or wonder why, at my time of life with a list of academic qualifications, I am doing what I am doing, I try to remind myself of the spirit that was Michael who found something here, in the rows and rows of books, that fed his remarkable soul.

Requiescat in pace Michael.

Through the glass

Margaret Mary, a member of staff, has a gift for window-dressing. She seems to take immense pleasure in thinking up what artefacts go with what annual festival or anniversary. And people do stop and look at her window. I often wish I could read the thoughts of people as they do this. In a perfect world the thoughts would suddenly appear in a balloon floating just over their heads like they are in cartoons. It would save me guessing. I wouldn't want it to happen the other way though. It wouldn't do for people to realise how nosy I am. So, until some kind of neuroscientific breakthrough happens, I have to be content with quietly observing the random folk who peer into our windows lost in private thought.

There was, for example, the old chap who must have spent the best part of twenty minutes slowly scanning his eyes over the display. Over the books wrapped in brown paper asking the viewer to guess their titles from the literary clues handwritten across them, over the red rose lying alluringly across a book spine, over the velvet heart propped against a book support, over the scarlet bow and string of dancing cupids, up to the cute collection of best loved love poems, across the two volumes of *Love Letters of Great Men / Women* — yes, those that Sarah Jessica Parker gushed over in *Sex and the City* — and coming finally to rest on the little teddy bear sitting in the corner of the window which asks 'Will You Be My Valentine?' I am not near enough to see the old chap's eyes. Judging though by the stillness of him, his eyes have misted over or gone blank. He is not here. He is away, years back, walking the braes with his lass, bending down to pluck a few fragile snowdrops for her to weave into her hair, hopeful of a kiss in return. Did the lass think him fine and handsome. Did he manage to woo her into saying 'Yes'? Did they then have many many more years stravaiging together in the bright February air? I watch and wonder. He suddenly sighs. Straightens up. Squares his cap more firmly on his head and walks slowly out of sight. I hope he is someone's dad, someone's dear old pal, someone's brother, someone's something, dear enough for someone to show they care on this day of declared love. What was it Burns wrote ? or at least collected?

My heart is sair — I dare na tell,

My hear is sair for Somebody;

I could wake a winter night

For the sake o' Somebody.

O—hon! for Somebody!

O—hey! for Somebody!

I could range the world around,

For the sake o' Somebody.

We all want to be a Somebody for Someone.

So, Margaret Mary's window dressing skills do more than just sell books. They prompt reveries, impressions, possibilities, do what windows in shops used to do i.e. advertise, entertain, amuse and remind people of special days and calendar festivals.

Sometimes her decorations are not to my taste if they incline towards emulating globalised American practices — such as the increasing adoption of the phraseology 'Trick or Treat' which is fast replacing the

Scots 'guising'. Indulge me in a short detour please ... I need to air a perennial soapboxer because it worries me that a generation of our kids are now growing up believing that they deserve to be given money, or something edible, just for the act of being in disguise. The long held Scottish tradition is that not only should the kids have made a good effort at a masquerade, but also they have to earn their haul by offering entertainment with a song, story, poem, dance, trick or joke. It is not about dressing up, going from house to house to collect sticky sweet stuff and if, finding a resident who does not wish to join in, setting their pampas grass on fire in retribution. That just isn't our way. That's just not good behaviour and, in full knowledge that I now sound like a Grumpy Old Woman, I ain't accepting it.

The differing practices stem, I am now going to argue, from the different concepts of the uncanny. Spiritualism or mesmerism, which came in from America to England (and I mean England), in the mid-nineteenth century, viewed the supernatural world as containing a strong element of the diabolic and was naturally to be feared. Similarly, the gothic tradition as favoured by Mary Shelley's *Frankenstein* (1818), Emily Bronte's *Wuthering Heights* (1847), Charlotte Bronte's *Jane Eyre* (1847) and George Eliot's *The Lifted Veil* (1859) with their emphasis on bleak moorlands, crumbling sinister houses and creepy ancient servants, can still be seen as clear influences upon contemporary English writers of the supernatural such as Susan Hill's acclaimed gothic novel, *The Woman in Black* (1983).

By contrast, what happens in Scotland's literature is something rather different. It is different because much of Scotland has been influenced by the ancient celtic understanding of the uncanny which, instead of being eradicated by the newer religion of Christianity, had been incorporated into it. An illustration of this fusion can be found in the Rev Robert Kirk's manuscript *The Secret Commonwealth of Elves, Fauns, and Fairies* (1691) and a further example in Alexander Carmichael's

Carmina Gadelica (1900) or its Gaelic title, *Ortha nan Gaidheal*, with its impressive listing of prayers, hymns, charms and incantations for all living things both human and non-human. Similarly, it is interesting to note that in Margaret Oliphant's short story 'The Open Door' (1882), it is the old Church of Scotland minister who recognises the agonised wail of an unseen spirit as belonging to that of a young lad searching for his mother and while the rational medical doctor and distinguished army Colonel hide quivering, the minister exhorts God to 'draw him in ower', and the presence disappears. In contemporary writing from Scotland — such as that by Kenneth Steven, Kathleen Jamie and Andrew Greig — this seamless blending of the tangible world around us and the not so tangible, is prevalent. Other landmark Scottish writers too — Hogg, Scott, Burns, Stevenson, Oliphant, Spark — to name but few, had been brought up since infancy with the oral ballads and stories and tales of 'the fairy folk' and 'the glamourie' which existed unseen all around and, now and again, could be glisked. Such rich cultural heritage undercutting all that flowed from their pen. In other words, the world of the supernatural in Scottish belief, wasn't necessarily something to be feared, wasn't necessary something of the Devil (and if it was he was usually found constructed as a rather charming and disarming gentleman — see Hogg's *Confessions of a Justified Sinner* (1824), James Bridie's *Mr Bolfry* (1943) or James Robertson's *The Testament of Gideon Mack* (2006). The uncanny, unlike the daft practice of table-rapping as espoused by trans-Atlantic spiritualists wooed by the sensationalism of it all, was viewed in Scotland just as being there and not something to go searching for or calling up. It existed not just beyond the veil of this life but in and through this life and therefore not in the least 'Other' to our daily existence. When kids then dress up in disguise they are effectively taking on another form, an unknown but not necessarily a scary unknown. And just as the unseen spirits interweave in daily life so the kids, in our culture, entertain the householder instead of threatening them. What is real is therefore not opposed to what is not real, it just mixes.

Forbye all this academic exegesis of the origins of Halloween (or Samhain in the Gaelic), I tend to find that if you insist on 'a turn' from each guiser, you will get one. And they are often a talented crew. Last year a wee Cinderella played me two tunes on my piano, a pint-size axe-wielding Devil turned a pretty good cartwheel, an Image of Death (hiding well behind his sister) sang an almost inaudible song but song it still was, and a whole host of cartoon characters, a medieval knight, an Egyptian slave, and a Where's Wally? recited a bit poetry and told me a lot of awful jokes. In our street, they've also come to expect that 'you get to dook fur apples in that hoose' — which the kids take to with great joy and gusto. It's important then to know our own traditions, to know why we do what we do, and quite frankly, it compliments our national sense of wanting value for money if we get a bit amusement for the pokes of sweets, apples and small change we part with every year. And, at the end of the day, it's just great fun. The kids like it and feel that they have done Halloween properly. Whit's wrang wi that?

What doesn't happen properly in Cloisters is Christmas. Christmas, it seems to me, is just tolerated not celebrated. I'm not too sure why this is. It would be easy to say that the attitude is a reaction to the horrible commercialisation that tries to swamp a religious festival, but I really don't think this is to blame. Margaret Mary does her best and creates a window with cotton wool snow, a cheery Santa, messages wishing the peerer-inner 'A Happy Christmas', tempts the peerer with a comforting 'Classics' sets of Dickens, Austen, Trollope or Scott — which are still popular despite the latest e-book reader already wrapped under trees at home. And the shop closes on Christmas Day and Boxing Day. But that's it really. Kelvin opts for the 'bah humbug' method of observance. But I, strange person that I am, like Christmas and therefore refuse to buckle under to scepticism or cynicism or any other negativism floating about. And, if you dig a little, I find that Christmas has a way of seeping into the shop anyway. Knowing now that little will be initiated by the management, I content myself with watching out for flashes of Christmas grace. And they come.

'Here. Here. These ur fur youse. I nicked them frae the work. They miserable bastards'll no miss them.'

The speaker is a chap whom I have silently dubbed 'Mr Sunshine'. He comes in every few weeks or so. Moans from the moment he gets inside the door about his work, the school kids on the bus, the local council, the neighbours, the local council, his doctor, the local council and society in general. We usually stem the flow by offering him a cup of tea. He likes tea not coffee and he likes the fact that we remember that. And he likes the fact that we listen to him, admire his drawings (which are rather good), and remember one or two details about his life. He never stays very long as he likes to 'get up the road afore they kids come oot,' but it's probably more that he's tired from his long shift in a factory and still has an uphill cycle home. I get the impression he has little money. His hours keep being cut — in some ways he likes this as it gives him more time to draw, but it also means his weekly budget is tight. The fistful of Quality Street chocs that he dumps down on the coffee tray is his way of saying thanks to us. It's rough, but it's full of grace. Yeh, they're nicked, but I'm not going to question the rights or wrongs or his action. It's based on kindness and that's all that matters. And anyway, I haven't a clue where he works, don't intend to ask and, judging by the fact that he is paying for a collection of graphic novels in instalments, tells me that his employers probably are 'miserable bastards' right enough.

Another moment of grace occurs in the days between Christmas and New Year. I'm back at work but have assuaged the possible gloom of that by instituting a wee tea party in the shop. I've invited some pals, some cheery and musical pals, to come. These pals are mostly teachers in some form or other which means (a) they're all enjoying a decent paid holiday and (b) are normally too busy to come to the bookshop. They all like the thought of a 'Carolling in the Bookshop' event as it appeals to a sense of nostalgia for a good old fashioned Christmas happening. My husband is also off on holiday and is more than happy to help ferry tins of biscuits, mince pies, pints of milk, napkins, plates and cups to the shop in anticipation of a good-going afternoon. Kelvin is around the shop in the morning but announces he is going home before 'the craziness' begins. I worry a little that he doesn't feel welcome but then decide that he's an adult, and the owner of the shop to boot, so presume he would stay if he wanted too. He does say though that my robin-red checked tablecloth is 'quite classy' so I guess he is fine with the jamboree. My pals are also readers and are all bringing their respective family members with Christmas money wearing a hole in their pockets. On the level of a business opportunity my afternoon soirée should be a definite plus.

'Did you survive the farce that is Christmas?' calls Pete, an occasional customer, as he comes through the door. He thinks he's being cool and right on. He is saying what he thinks we want to hear.

I don't bother to argue but simply reply 'Coffee? Mince pie? Music?'

'Whit's all this?' he asks bemused.

'Christmas cheer,' I say.

He looks from me to the table which is now littered with two teapots, a coffee pot, cakes, sweet things and carol sheets. My pals are in the middle of belting out 'When Santa Got Stuck Up The Chimney' — and those who aren't playing an instrument are singing with great glee.

'Aw no, I've a doctor's appointment. I can't stay,' says Pete.

'No worries. But have a mince pie before you go,' I urge.

He watches the scene for a few moments and as the 'band' close their number he saunters over to the table.

I introduce him to some of the folks. Someone pours him a coffee, shoves a plate of chocolate fingers at him.

'C'mon, join in, I'm Maisie,' she says.

He starts to say that he can't stay but then changes that to:

'Maybe just a quick coffee and wee biscuit … and maybe one of those mince pies … That's a good sound, I like Yamaha guitars … Eh, well, aye I do play a bit … but … aye … ok then.'

And he's away. The doctor's appointment is forgotten. He displays some deft finger work on my pal's guitar, gets applause, does another then another. Gives back the guitar, takes another cake, another coffee, sits back and croons along to 'I'm Dreaming of a White Christmas'. Some two hours later he finally leaves the shop. Happy.

'Same time, same place next year then, eh?' he says to my pals.

The farce that is Christmas?

While this was going on another wee vignette took place. Another regular had swayed in, reeking of his favourite hostelry. He's a nice chap. Always polite and calm. He looks amused at the shenanigans going on but stays on track and asks if he can check out a book he has ordered, that has arrived in the shop, but he can't yet pay for.

I bring it to the counter and we look at it together. It's a study of three graphic artists. The artwork is excellent. Had life been different for this customer, art could have been his life. I've seen some of his own work and it's not half bad. I think on Gray's line 'Full many a flower born to blush unseen …,' but then question if this chap's life has really been 'wasted on the desert air'? There is still a sweetness in how he does what he does.

We close the book. He turns to smile at the singers — my friends and husband are now for some reason bellowing out 'Rawhide'. An unknown in the Christmas carol repertoire but perhaps it is the lesser for it.

'Good sounds,' says my customer.

He then suddenly lifts my hand, kisses it, smiles again and trots off to his vacated seat in the pub.

Fou and skint, but nevertheless a veritable Christmas gentleman.

Too True Crime

It's mid afternoon and there are a handful of customers in the shop. One is over at Health, one is up at Religion, one is at either Philosophy or Physics — it's hard to tell from my standpoint — and there are two in the Crime vault. I'm working through a box of poetry pamphlets, checking their condition and listing them on the bookshop web page. It's footerie work as the job had been started by the two school lads we'd had in for work experience. The boys were wonderfully enthusiastic — one of them providing high entertainment with his rendition of Russian songs — but the fine tuning required for various tasks wasn't quite what they were interested in. Some close checking of their efforts with the poetry pamphlets is required. This is the kind of job you can only do when none of our 'Regular Blethers' — as Serena, a member of staff has dubbed them — are delighting us with their company. When they are in, bless them, they seem to think that hanging over the counter and sharing their latest theories on life and the universe, is a fitting supplement to the poor owner or staff member valiantly trying to focus on the world of bookselling. This afternoon however, praise be, none of them have so far appeared. The poetry listing is going well.

The two people who were in Crime, come over to the counter. The woman is carrying a pile of Stephen King books. We exchange pleasantries — not about Stephen King, I'm not too well read on him — but on how good it is to really get into an author you like. It's bitterly cold outside and I say that I can think of nothing nicer on an afternoon like this than a hot brew, a comfy armchair, a toasty fire and a great book. We all linger on the image even though it is highly likely that none of us can do the 'roaring fire' bit due to having central heating instead of a more aesthetically pleasing form, but it sounds nice. I ring the books up and am handing the bulging bag to the woman, when her man says:

'Em … ah don't suppose you hiv heard of a book cried *Gangs of Dundee*?'

'*Gangs of Dundee*?' I echo, 'I don't think so, but if we have it here it would possibly be with other books on Dundee in the Scottish section, just there, or … it's not True Crime is it?'

'Aye, hen, it's totally true,' he says grinning.

'In that case it might be on the True Crime shelves up there,' I say, gesturing towards the front of the shop.

We keep the True Crime books separate from Fictional Crime for reasons born of experience. True Crime can attract what my mum would term 'an element' of society and it's sensible therefore to have such books near the shop door so to discourage too much loitering around areas of the shop hidden from view. As it usually turns out though, customers interested in this genre are often quite fascinated by it, and will stand for a good half hour reading through titles and flicking through to the graphic photographs often contained therein. I tend to show such customers where the books are then leave them to it. Decapitated and charred bodies of victims and haunted faces of the killers, aren't my field.

I show the chap where he might find *Gangs of Dundee* saying that it wasn't a title I was familiar with, but one never knew what you could find, and begin to move back to the till point.

He doesn't look at the shelves but says 'You see, ah've got dyslexia, and that's the only book ah hiv read right through, every word, in ma puff'.

'I hope you enjoyed it,' I say.

'Ah did that,' he says 'because ah knew some of they lads in it.'

'Is that right?' I say sensing a monologue coming on and moving back another few steps.

'Aye,' he says, moving after me. 'And ah'll tell ye how ah knew theim. Ah wis in a gang maself. Ah knew all aboot gang life. And ah tell ye, whoever wrote that book got it right, so he did. Not that ma gang wisnae unique, we wur. We wur special. We ruled the streets then. Thoosands of us. The police boys didnae know whit tae dae wi us.'

'And to look at you, you seem a right decent person,' I say, hoping to move the emphasis back to respectability and to reassure other, possibly worried, customers overhearing this conversation, that he didn't look like a raving axeman.

'Oh, aye, noo I am, but no then. Naw. I wis wild. Ah wis in the jile tae – twice – fur ma sins. And ah mean 'fur ma sins', ah know it wisnae right whit ah did, ah tell ma kids that,' he offers.

'Good for you,' I say, relieved to hear this.

'Aye. But oh, ah cin tell some stories.'

My insides groan and I smile and turn to go.

'Like when we went doon tae London, looking fur the Chelsea lads. They hid the reputation o being the toughest gang in Britain at the time. Well we didnae think so, so we went looking fur them. Aboot a hundred of us aw went.'

'That must have been quite a train journey.'

'Went by bus — cheaper. Mental it wis. Onyway, we went searching fur thae Chelsea lads and we fun them.'

'Really?'

'Aye, we fought them and they won. Ah hiv tae say they were good. They deserved their title. But ah came tae ma senses because o meeting them. Ah saw ma mate get whit they ca 'the Chelsea kiss' – they pit a machete in yer mouth and stamp on it.'

'Oh, don't!' I protest, my hands flying to my mouth.

'Aye, isnae nice. Ma mate lived though. But aifter that ah decided tae chuck the gang. I'd hud enough.'

'Ah'm glad to hear that,' I say, conscious of other, now possibly trembling, bodies in the shop.

'But ah wid still like tae get that book though. It wis a good read,' the chap says. 'Telt ye all aboot how yer gangmates were brothers. Ye know they say that Scotland wis really racist years ago, but ah tell ye, see if ye were in a gang, didnae matter wit colour yer skin wis, ye were a brother and that wis that. Total acceptance. Total.'

'Um … that was one good thing, I suppose.'

'Aye. Total. Anyway, hen, nice talking tae ye. Ah'll pop in again.'

He turns to his patiently waiting wife.

'C'mon doll, we'd better get up the road fur the granweans comin oot the schule. I don't want tae be late fur them. Disnae look good. Cheerio hen.'

And off they saunter.

As I watch them move out of the doorway, I become aware that there is absolutely no movement from the other customers in the shop.

A short chaser

The shop door jangles and a large man reels up to the counter. He is sartorially challenged and looks like he's just tipped off a bar stool and is working his way back towards it.

'Can I help you sir?' I enquire in a brisk but non-challenging tone.

He grins at me in what my mother would call 'a daft way'. His brain appears to be attempting to register my question and begin the challenging process of working out an answer. He seems to be having trouble with the procedure. I smile at him and raise my eyebrows in the hope of enabling the process.

He looks at me for a moment longer, his features twisted into thought, then says:

'Aw, it's jist nice tae be asked that by a fuckin fine-lookin wummin.'

His brain, happy that some words have been issued, now turns him around and he walks, slowly and carefully back down the aisle, holding out his arms on both sides as if in a moving train, tugs open the door and sways out into the street.

Sometimes there are no words.

Obfuscation

-   So how does it work then?

-   Sorry, what works?

-   This place. How does it work?

-   Em … we're a bookshop.

-   A bookshop. Not a library?

-   No. A bookshop.

-   So I can't borrow books?

-   No. But you can buy them.

-   Buy them?

-   Yes. It's a shop.

-   A shop … So how does it work then?

Code Cracker

I see this book is £2.50.

Yes. It's part of a set. Would you like to see the other volu....

It says £2.50 here but there's a strange thing below that. Says 'S 48'. What's that?

Oh, that's just a shop code so we know how long it's been on the shelves.

Who's 'S'? You?

No, not me.

What's your initial?

Ah, that would be telling.

Ok. But, the '48', what does that mean?

That's the month.

So ... if it's 48 that means that you've been open ... four years?

Yes.

Tazah! I've cracked the bookshop code! Bye!

Still Cooking

It's one of those quiet Monday afternoons. Kelvin has already gone home with the vague plan of 'a snooze, a fruit smoothie and a run'. At least I think that's what he said, he perhaps meant the other way around, but knowing Kelvin, probably not. Anyway, it's almost 3.30 and thus time to put the kettle on. Occasionally, if the shop is quietish — and only if, so don't pop in on a crazy day and expect this — I go round the aisles asking if anyone would like a cuppa. If there are enough takers I make a pot of tea, sit it on the table under its warm red cosy, drop an assortment of paper cups or ceramic mugs beside it, bring the sugar and milk over and shout 'Tea's up folks!' It's amusing for me to watch the random grouping that sometimes happens. A university professor, a retired or active musician, a struggling or not so struggling artist, sitting down with whatever one of our Frequent Flyers is hanging about, or with the man waiting for a call from the garage to say his car is ready or with the couple who have been paying their final respects at the Crematorium, or with the folk who make a day trip to the shop from Arran, or those sent round to us by the auction room people. Despite their differences, they always find some common ground to talk about.

This afternoon there is just one customer in. He's up at Cookery. I clocked him coming in some ten minutes ago but, as I recognised him as someone who knew the shop, I had left him alone. It's shop policy though to make some gesture of communication with all customers even if the briefest of 'hi' and 'goodbye'. So even while hurtling through cleaning and coding a pile of popular kids' authors — Roald Dahl, Francesca Simon, Meg Cabot — I had registered his presence and factored in some contact in the next few minutes. Stuffing the now cleaned books into their appropriate places on the shelves, I then made my way up to Cookery.

'Are you alright there?' I call, 'Would you like a wee cup of tea?'

I'm deliberately calling quite loudly as I remember this customer as rather a frail old chap with a hearing aid. Kelvin had dealt with him last time when the chap had tottered up to the counter with a hardback *Reader's Digest* compendium saying that he had found it behind books on Roman history. We use such compendiums to prop up other books as *Reader's Digest* are themselves of useless saleable quality — please take note of that and don't even think about dumping them with us.

'Eh don't think it should be theyah,' the old chap had chuckled, pleased to have found a possible stacking flaw.

Kelvin didn't have the heart to say 'You dopey old codger! Put it back, we need it there,' but had politely thanked him and quietly put it back later.

Now, following my question about tea, the old chap shuffles round to face me and says:

'Oh, eh'm fine thenk you. Quite quite heppy. And I won't have tea. It's awfully kend of you but it would make me Go, you know?'

Ah yes. Old bladders and all that. I'll need to be quiet slurping my own tea then. Don't want any associated connotations happening.

It is cold outside but the old boy is muffled and buttoned and clipped up to face the meanest of weathers. I wonder that the weight of his sheepskin coat isn't too much for his vulnerable body or that his small but bulging backpack — tethered across his chest with the strap which I have only seen deployed on the most serious of trekker's backpacks — isn't keeling him backwards. His parchment thin skin stretched over his high-cheekboned face and veined neck looks as if it could easily be punctured by too much pressure.

'Aye see ye lookin' at my backpack,' he says.

Oops, was I that obvious?

'It's full of electrical things eh just got from that shop along there. So eh've no space today to carry any books. So eh'm just going to look today, if that's alright?'

I tell him that of course that's fine and that we can always put anything aside for him if he wants.

'Well, eh might take this another time,' he says.

He waves a small paperback at me. It could easily fit in his backpack but I judge that another ounce of weight could be the fatal straw. I'm about to say that I could leave it behind the counter for him, when he goes on.

'Yes, eh'm really a Science man, but eh hev to say, this looks quite useful. Maybe just the thing.'

The book is *Cooking for Blokes*.

'I suppose cooking is a kind of science too,' I say and, thinking that that ends my 'Be helpful to customers' bit, turn to go. But there's more.

'Yes, that's what I told mayh wife. She did all the cooking when she was alive — except once. It was very strange you know, we were in our caravan, yes, yes, eh thenk it must have been the caravan, and she suddenly said 'You can cook the meal this evening'. Eh think she thought eh would make a fuss because she had never seen me cook. But what she forgot was that my mother had diyed when eh was fefteen and eh had to help in the house and so eh had learned a few skills to help my father. So anyway, eh cooked the meal and at the end she said 'Well, that was really quite tasty'. Eh think she was surprised. She never asked me again though. Eh don't really know why she did that time.'

I consider saying it may have saved him from being battered to death by a meat-cleaver by a bored out-of-her-mind woman. He might judge that a tad rude though, so I don't.

He goes on.

'It's funny though, eh never really liked her. Not sure if she really liked me. She diyed two years ago.'

'And do you miss her?'

'Eh suppose eh do, a bit, but … you know eh've met a girrulll.'

'A girrull? Eh … a girl?' My mind starts expanding and contracting trying to position the possible age or image of this female.

'Yes. Eh was walking up to the Centre …'

Centre? Day care?

'… and eh caught sight of her through the window. And, do you know? Eh thought she looked like a goddess!'

'A … goddess?'

'Yes, a goddess!'

'That, of course, is what all women want to hear.'

'But no, no, she really is! And my friend thenks so too. And that surprised me because when eh went into the Centre she was in the middle of giving my friend a right good telling off. Eh thought he would be furious, but when he turned towards me he was saying 'Beautiful. Oh, so beautiful.'

'Really?'

Sod the tea. This is good stuff. I rest my elbow on a nearby bookcase and flip open the part of my mind marked, 'Very useful material', and settle in for a good glean.

'And did you speak to her?'

I feel like a wummin windae-hingin. Determined not to miss an infinitesimal amount of information.

'Of course. And, eh hev to say, she seemed to really take to me. We had a great chat and whenever eh go there she makes a beeline for me.'

I'm now wondering if he is at that stage of male dementia when repressed libido, kept under bolts for the length of a long respectable marriage, can suddenly erupt. When I was a young student I spent some of my summer holidays doing voluntary in a hospice and well, let's just say some of the old guys there didn't hold back on attempting to express their thoughts, verbally and physically, on the female staff. But this chap doesn't seem dotty, at least I don't think so. I could be wrong. I need some more info to ascertain.

'That's nice for you,' I say a little patronisingly.

'Oh, eh just adore her! Eh really do! Eh never thought eh would ever feel like this or meet someone like her at my age. What age do you think eh am?'

Truthful answer is 96 but I opt for the ego-flattering 'Early 70s'. Och, why not?

He smiles a wee-boy-got-sweeties-smile, and says triumphantly 'Eh'm 86!'

'My goodness,' I simper, 'that's amazing.'

'Mmphm. So maybe it's not too late for me.'

'Never too late,' I cliché. Well, it's not, is it? Is it?

'That's what others have said.'

So, there are other liars out there too.

'But eh'm a bit worried that someone's said to her that eh'm interested in mahridge. She hasn't been around to see me for a wee while. Eh think that Morag — my home help — has been gossiping. Maybe she's put her off me.

'And are you interested in mahridge, em, marriage?' I say

'Oh yes. Eh love her! And, ye know, eh've got money. Eh've got lots of money and a big house.'

'Have you told her that?' I ask. I mean, how bad could it be ... old chap, loaded, maybe meet his maker soon ... ?

'No, eh thought she ...'

' ... should like ... em ... love ... you for yourself?' I finish.

'That's it. But do you think eh should tell her about the money?'

'Hell yeh!' is my first thought. But I say 'Maybe you should try to see her a bit more first. See if you're right for each other.' I have to give the lassie a bit of a chance for decent ethics. 'How about asking her to something? A meal?'

'Eh could, but she's married so it's a wee bit difficult for her and ...'

'She's married?' Stop the bus. This is a totally other scenario.

'Yes. Yes. But that's just a wee hitch. Eh don't think she likes her husband. She could get out of it.'

The randy old lad. Maybe I should go and make the tea and leave him to it — don't want him turning his attentions on me. But I guess by now he must have put me in the 'non-goddess' category. I think I'm quite safe. I shift my weight a bit. This chap's incredible. Or maybe I should give him the benefit of doubt. Maybe she is a stunner. Maybe she does like the older, much older, man. Maybe her husband is a total bore. And isn't life for living till you die? By the look of this chap we may be talking next Tuesday.

'So, you'll need to plot your next move carefully. Make her an offer she can't refuse.' I want to say 'Try £500,000,' but resist.

His pale blue eyes twinkle and they seem to suddenly have a far away look. Or is that just cataracts?

'Yes. Yes. Eh'll have a good think about it on the train.'

'Maybe you'll meet her on the train? Maybe she'll be sitting there when you get on. Serendipity and all that.'

'Oh, that would be nice,' he says, and if rheumatic old geezers can bounce, he suddenly bounces up and down on his soft sole Clarks lace-ups.

'Eh think eh'll go now,' he says, grinning. 'Got to catch a train.'

He puts *Cooking For Blokes* down on a pile of aircraft magazines.

'This is quite good, but eh don't really think eh need it.'

'No,' I say. 'I somehow don't think you do.'

He moves towards the exit taking small careful steps, holding on to whatever prop he can find. I skip past him and pull open our hefty door — somehow I think it would defeat even his indefatigable spirit .

'Thenk you,' he says 'eh'll let you know what happens.'

'And I'll look forward to that,' I say.

As he passes over the doorstep I hear him beginning to hum. The tune is 'Some Enchanted Evening'. I find myself smiling.

To See Oursels As Ithers See Us

There are occasions in the bookshop when one has to put one's belief in one's literary knowledge in one's back pocket because, in the eyes of a customer, it just simply doesn't wash. Like the time a chap came in the shop and asked me if we had anything by Jim Thompson.

'Um. Jim Thompson?' I queried. 'What kind of thing does he write?'

This is always my fallback question and I have learned it is always worth the asking. Failure to ask it means a pointless spin around the shelves with no idea of what I am looking for.

'Jim Thompson? Jim Thompson? He does aw that crime and pulp stuff. Well he did. He's deid now.

Ah, a fusion of fields. Hands up. I know very little about this genre and it's possibly true that I want to know very little about it. But at least I should be able to point him in the right direction.

'In that case, if we have him, he'll either be in Crime or Fiction,' I say leading the way into the Crime vault and gesturing at the floor-to-ceiling shelving up the left hand wall.

'That's great, hen, thanks. I'll hiv a look here. So you've no heard of him?' the chap says.

'No, I haven't,' I confess.

'Are ye no really a book person then?' he asks.

I hesitate a moment, my formal literary qualifications jingle in my ears.

'No, no really,' I say.

'S'all right, we cannae be good at everything,' he comforts, patting me on the arm.

Like to Like

They're blue-white skinny with jerky nervy muscle movements. One
has a healed razor slash on his face. They go over to Military History.
These are the type of customer that makes me see the wisdom in moving
up to the front of the shop near the door and pretend to sort the First
Look table. I keep an eye on the counter, check every ten seconds that
my phone and keys are in my pocket. There are some situations it could
pay to be canny. After eight minutes or so one of them comes and stands
at the counter. I take a breath, lower my shoulders and tell myself to be
brave. I call from halfway down the corridor:

'All right there sir?'

'Aye' he says, turning towards me, 'Jist want tae buy this please.'

He's making no suspicious movements and has money in his hand.
I decide he's ok. The book is something on conspiracy theory — which
usually lends itself to some discussion on what's going on in the world
that us, mere punters, don't all know about but which the customer
actually does and is the only person on the planet (and perhaps the
author of the said book too) who is aware and about to blow the whistle.
I've learned not to comment on the choice of such a book. Life's too
short.

As I'm ringing up the till his pal who has come over and loitered near
Scottish fiction, bends down and says to himself:

'*Fiiilth*' — whit's that?'

I purse my lips to answer but his henchman gets there first.

'Aye, that's that yin that did *Trainspottin* … totally brilliant book that man, so it is. Made intae a film n aw.'

Without thinking I flip into my 'Defend Intelligent Scotland From The Eedyits' mode.

'You know,' I say forgetting that it really would be best to let these two go on their merry way, 'I really struggle a bit with how it depicts Scotland. I mean, we're not all drug-users and knifers are we?'

As the peelie-wally faces of the two lads look back at me I am suddenly acutely conscious of the irony.

'Aye,' says the one with the razor mark, 'Yer right. It's not a guid representation of us. We're no aw smack-heids.'

Aye, s'right,' says the other 'And hiv youse seen him on telly? Right miserable bastard. Aw that money frae these books and cannae raise a smile. Pitiful. Pitiful.'

'Ah weel, that's whit twinty year on heroin will dae fur ye,' says the other 'Jist makes ye a torn-faced git.'

I smile but remain silent. I suddenly feel out of my depth.

'Weel, we'd better get up the road,' says one.

'Aye, cheers, thanksalot. Might come back fur that *Trainspottin* though even if the writer's a pathetic job,' says the other.

'No probs,' I say, feeling my shoulders lower. 'See you again gentlemen.'

Angel Offensive

I wasn't quite listening at first. Kelvin was reading something out loud from the diary. Reading in that kind of way which is more in the manner of checking something over and not intended as a performance piece.

' "Took books. Left with ward staff." Right. That's done. Hope she likes them.'

Having no idea of what the note concerns and aware that there is really little point in asking — Kelvin likes to feed the staff stories only when he is ready — I carried on shoving more Eoin Colfer stories onto their usual shelf which had dramatically emptied itself following an enthusiastic buyer.

A half hour later, while I was still attempting to create order in Children — a school class had graced the shop with a visit since I had last been on duty — I heard the doorbell jangle and a bright voice call.

'Hallooo. Only me.'

Cassie.

I straightened myself up from the plastic boxes of books for pre-school kids which are stored on the floor so little hands can reach them, and peered round the shelves. I always like it when Cassie calls in. She's a bright and cheerful person even when in a stew about something, often comes bearing donations for our biscuit tin, is interested in the wider connectedness of all things, frequently buys or orders a book and will happily get involved in whatever random conversation is taking place on her arrival. She's popular with all of the staff as she understands that dialogue works better when each person gets a say, doesn't hing over the counter splurging a stream-of-consciousness as others do, and never outstays her welcome. Her appearance then invariably comes as light relief — particularly if I have just been treated to the company of more arbitrary minds.

Today Kelvin gets in first.

'Ah. Good. I have a job for you. Do you want a job?'

'A job? What kind of job?'

'Just answer the question.'

'Well, tell me about it. What do you want me to do?'

'Go to the hospital and see if the books we gave are suitable.'

'What books? Suitable with who? Whom?'

'Wait a minute. Wait. Wait. How will you know if you don't listen.'

I grin at Cassie and ask her if she would like some coffee. This could take a while. For some reason Kelvin delights in wrong-footing people. Conversation with him is a bit like a game of chess which all too rapidly moves to 'Check mate!' when all you have intended to do is either relate a simple tale or idly shoot the breeze. I therefore tend to warn anyone whom I know that intends to visit the shop for the first time, especially more sensitive souls, that any opening gambit made or casual remark about the weather, the bookshop, the book trade or whatever, is liable to be caught, shredded and flung back at the speed of sound. Kelvin you see, gets great enjoyment from the ancient practice of 'flyting' — a pastime and spectator sport popular in the Scottish royal court a few centuries ago which involved the trading of insults. And, if truth be told, it's precisely his honed skill at this recreation that attracts many of the Regular Blethers who view the scathing syllables that issue out of Kelvin's mouth as a game which fills their barren souls with sheer delight. When a particular choice morsel of blatant bluntness has been hurled, an RB will grin appreciatively as if witnessing a match-winning shot at Wimbledon. But mostly, once customers are used to the sport, they simply ignore the baiting and wait patiently until the layer of 'How to speak nicely to people' which was surely instilled in him by his mammie, rises to the surface.

This is precisely what Cassie does, accepting my offer of coffee and a biscuit then moving across to the table to chat with me for a minute or two. Realising he isn't going to get anywhere by his usual method, Kelvin comes over and tries another tact.

'Seeing as you have got nothing to do (Cassie lets that pass even though she has just come back from her daily visit to her elderly mum in her care home), would you like to visit a hospital?'

'Why?' says Cassie sipping her coffee, a twinkle of amusement in her eye.

'American woman. Broken hip. Niece asked for books for her. Serena took them. Need to know if she wants more. Ok?'

This time it is Cassie's turn to say 'Wait. Wait. What?'

'I've just told you. American woman. Broken hip. Niece asked for books. Serena took them. Need to know if she wants more. How hard can this be?'

Cassie looks at me. I shrug my shoulders having no more information than she.

'How did she break her hip? And why is she in our hospital?'

'Questions. Questions. I've got a shop to run. Ok. OK. The backstory … are you listening? Right. Woman in Iona — no, don't know why — falls, taken to the hospital, stranger here, niece in Canada searches net, finds us, emails to request books for her aunt — memoirs and stuff. Serena takes them. I need to know if she wants more or if the books are ok. Want the job? Her name is Clare and she's in Ward 22.'

'Ok,' says Cassie.

'Visiting hours on this bit of paper,' says Kelvin, 'but you could always blast in and say you're on a mission of mercy.'

'I'll go this afternoon — at the proper time,' says Cassie.

'And remember to report back,' says Kelvin 'No point in leaving the job half done.'

'I'll come straight in here afterwards.'

'And make sure you get any messages correct,' says Kelvin and goes off to resume his seat of power at the till.

True to her word Cassie comes back into the shop later in the afternoon. She feeds us the full back story which is that the American lady is actually English but has been a long term resident in the US. She has a broken hip due to falling backwards having been startled by a wee, sleekit, cow'rin tim'rous beastie (who was equally startled at being interrupted at his dinner) in a cupboard in her friend's house in Iona. There being no resident doctor on the island, one had to be ferried over from Mull who then decided to have Clare flown to the mainland. A long lull of a few hours then ensued as the now morphine-soothed Clare had to wait until the air ambulance dealt with more serious cases. This done, they came for her and bore her away to our town and its general hospital, where she landed vulnerable, worried, no clue where she was, without a friend or family member in easy reach.

More, and other slightly more random parts, of the back story are related and related again as Cassie takes it upon herself to visit the stranded woman every couple of days.

'Guess what?' says Cassie after one of the visits. 'She's right into the six degrees of separation. We'd a great blether. She's really very interesting. And she's written a book about Iona. I need to get you to order it for me. And I told her you were a writer too, Anne. You've really got lots in common. You'd like her.'

By this time I am starting to feel a little guilty. I have done diddly-squat to help this woman. I reason to myself she has Cassie and that I have had visitors and a horrible cold. The shipwrecked woman — whom we now know as Clare — wouldn't want me sharing my bugs with her, would she now? My guilt increases when Cassie told me that Clare was in need of some laundry being done. Someone had brought her suitcase down from Iona but hadn't noticed a plastic bottle full of water inside. The bottle had spilled its contents over the clothes in the suitcase which were now in a distinctly stourie state. There apparently is no hospital service for those patients who have no nearby relatives or friends who can take home their grubby washing and bring it back cleansed. Yes, daft. Just how are unplanned patients supposed to cope? Anyway, Cassie, being Cassie, despite the fact she has no washing machine and no outside drying facility, took Clare's dirty clothes home (by bus), hand-washed them, sprinkled lavender oil in the rinse water, hung them up to dry in her wee flat, took them back, ironed and folded beautifully. I have a washing machine, I have a back garden with a whirly-gig, I live within walking distance from the hospital. But I didn't do Clare's washing. Cassie did.

This story came into the mind of my husband a few days later while he stood in a posh suburb of Edinburgh trying to find the phone number of a local taxi firm. Asking the help of a newsagent, a pub and a cafe, but receiving zero heed or help, he finally located one himself. As he was carried off towards his next appointment — now late — he reflected on the story of Cassie doing a stranger's washing. Tasteful, expensive suburb of an elegant city set against our less than pretty, hard up and often besmirched town, he knew which one he was glad he was living in.

The days rumbled on. Cassie regularly reported on Clare's condition and their shared conversation. I knew that Cassie was probably disappointed I hadn't visited Clare — truth to tell I was disappointed in myself. But I had a part-time job to do, writing, reviewing and tutoring to do, a house to run, visitors, dogs and a house and a man and a son to look after, and all that gallimaufry or so I told myself.

Kelvin even visited. Kelvin! Knowing all too well his belief in what was appropriate conversation for customer care in the bookshop I really wondered just how suitable his bedside manner for a sick stranger might be. I wasn't sure if Clare or the nursing staff would cope. But maybe it would provide them with some new form of entertainment.

He tells me that he is taking a bottle of Lucozade to the woman. He recites a story of some lass stricken down with a mysterious energy sapping ailment who was advised by a doctor to sip Lucozade when she felt tired. Apparently it worked miracles, so Kelvin believes a glug of this sickly-sweet E number laden drink might just be the missing ingredient in the local hospital's care package. I have my doubts. We now know, having googled her, that Clare is a Professor Emerita of Landscape Architecture at the University of California, and author of studies such as *Housing as if People Mattered* (1992), *House as Mirror of Self* (2007), *Therapeutic Landscapes* (2013) as well as her memoir *Iona Dreaming* (2010). This prestigious publishing list suggests an educated lifestyle. I wonder how she will cope with a ubiquitous west of Scotland taste experience. Perhaps the gesture will be at least be appreciated.

I go out at lunchtime in search of comforting soup. I really do have a lingering cold and, as the bookshop temp averages cool even in the hottest of days, I feel the need of warmth.

'Sit in, talk to people and bring back interesting stories,' orders Kelvin — which is his way of showing he cares about his staff.

Armed with that mission I do just that. I first of all call at the newsagent – or 'the 2B pencil shop' as Kelvin has dubbed it. The woman in there is sharp and is always a source of what's happening in her end of town. Currently she's on a crusade to get Kelvin to look at a vacant shop unit across the road from her shop. It's next to the library which is next to the museum, so it would definitely work as far as footfall is concerned. Parking though could be a slight problem and then there is also the small practicality of moving the thousands of books in the existing shop. (Ye gods. Whenever I think of this I make a mental note to call in sick that week). Being but a lowly staff member I have of course absolutely no remit to discuss this, but don't let a triviality such as that stop me. The 2B shop woman and I therefore confer about the bookshop moving until another customer demands her attention. Soup calls and I trot on to the café.

It occurs to me that my husband may also be on a lunch break and so I dial his work number. My intuition was right and ten minutes later he joins me in the café where I have ordered spicy red pepper soup and two gluten-free tuna pieces and a pot of Earl Grey tea. (I hear your surprise but our town does have a quiet classy cultured side if you are prepared to search for it.) We chomp and blether catching up on our respective mornings. I tell him of Kelvin's plan to visit the American woman that afternoon. My husband says that this will further amaze the woman who must already be wondering just what lengths our customer service will stretch to.

Truth is that we are all quite enjoying building this illusion of benevolence and compassion. We also judge it quite sound as the woman's plan is to leave the hospital in a few days and fly as straight home as a wheelchair bound passenger can. We're all a little relieved at this plan as we think that this will keep her image of the bookshop, as a place of true charity and our town as a harbour for the desperate, sufficiently water-tight. She need never see our disastrous high street with its tacky array of discount and charity shops or the shabby unchic of the street the bookshop is located in, nor experience the chat of the local intelligentsia.

My tum now cosy and full, I begin to gather my gear and as I do so my eye falls on the display of cakes behind the glass counter. There are three delicious and tasty looking 'Portuguese Cakes'. My mind flashes back to the various times I have found myself enjoying the menus of our local hospital. While keeping you alive (unless suffering from pancreatitis as I was and the proffered sausages and chips would have put an end to any need for further care as I would be dead), the dietary fare can err on the side of boring. Maybe some Proustian sweet cakes, might bring a smidgeon of cheer to this woman. I ask the assistant for the three of them and also ask for them to be put in a box. I have visions of a nice square cardboard box tied up with ribbon or string. She gives me a decidedly functional polystyrene carton, perhaps fine for a hot toastie but which falls completely short of any elegance. I thank her anyway, pay for the lunch and cakes, say goodbye to my other half —now chuckling at some story in the local paper — and leave the café.

My path takes me past an interior design shop where I buy scented candles from time to time. I wonder if they would have a better carrier for my gift. They do and I emerge some six minutes later with a neat multi-coloured box just perfect for carrying and enhancing the three cakes which are now safe inside surrounded by pink tissue paper. My sense of style and decorum are satisfied.

Back at the bookshop I give Kelvin the swanky wee box.

'Oh right, show me up, why don't you?' he says. 'Me with my man-present and you with your ultra-feminine thoughtful one.'

'Just tell her it represents the yin and yang of the bookshop,' I retort. 'But take them anyway.'

He does so and trots off later having carefully calculated just how much of the visiting hour would be appropriate for him to inflict his company on. I am quite sure that Cassie is also visiting this afternoon but refrain from telling Kelvin this. I think it will be an amusing scene for Cassie to witness and anyway I need an acute observer to report back to me. I smile to myself at the thought of what the ward staff must be thinking. For someone who was flown in from the island where she was holidaying and who reportedly knew not a soul in our area, she certainly is accumulating visitors. Kelvin's wife, Mairéad, had also gone in to see her the day before and Cassie has become a regular bedside attendee. I wonder if we could put a small advert on the bookshop website with some wording to the effect that we can cater for the reading tastes of stranded and sick visitors to our town and can do personal delivery and regular visiting. Beat that, Amazon!

I get on with trying to cram more Scottish fiction into the already full shelves. Various customers come and go — one talking not of Michelangelo (that's a literary allusion not a typo), but of Renoir and Moira Shearer in one breath — and then the shop doorbell clashes. It's Cassie looking breathless and amused.

'Hey, how went the tea party?' I asked. 'Did Kelvin turn up?'

'Oh he did and oh he was in fine fettle and Clare was fair taken with him. They had a right good old talk. It was great fun. Just like being here but no books and no mad folk — well, apart from Kelvin.'

I get her some coffee and grab a pile of books to clean while she fills me in with more detail. I tell her of my idea of 'Books for the Shipwrecked'. She giggles but sees the potential.

'And,' I say, 'there's another gap in the market you could plunge into — 'Exclusive Laundry for the Desperate'. I reckon you could charge some astronomical price for your service of handwashing, with extra for a drop of lavender oil, extra for ironing and extra again for return delivery with the clothes bound in ribbon in a colour of the customer's choice.'

'Och you,' Cassie says sipping her coffee 'I was just happy to help Clare.'

'Aye, but maybe her appearance in your life is the first step to greater things,' I pursue. 'You could get a list of all the overseas people who suddenly find themselves guests of the hospital, go chat them up, get their laundry, buy a wee van with suitable signage, and ...voila! ... you're in business.'

'Or I could just keep coming here and enjoying myself,' counters Cassie giggling at my nonsense.

Well, one can only suggest, if she doesn't want such a lucrative business opportunity, then I'm keeping it up my sleeve. I could charge another extra for delivery of freshly cleaned clothes with a selection of reading material — suitable 'Sick Lit' of course — and a side order of Lucozade and ritzy cakes. Maybe onto something here.

It continued to nag me though that I had done next to nothing for our stranded academic. And, more than that, was the feeling that I was missing an opportunity. But an opportunity for what I wasn't quite sure. I finally decided to act on this feeling when Cassie told me that Clare was to be discharged and would be returning to California in a couple of days. When I got home that evening I said to my husband that I was entertaining the idea of popping up to the hospital.

'I'll come with you,' he said 'she sounds like an interesting person.'

So, go we did.

The ward was quiet when we got there and after asking one of the nurses where we might find 'Clare, the American lady ... broken hip ...', we were directed to a bay where a grey-haired woman was quietly sitting in one of those high-backed hospital chairs beside her bed.

I smiled and went towards her announcing:

'Hi. I'm from Cloisters Bookshop. I'm the one who sent you the cakes. I just thought I'd come and see you before you went home — and this is my husband.'

Clare looked slightly startled but, smoothing down her dressing-gown, said some opening polite things and asked us to take a seat.

We left well after the bell to signal the end of Visiting Hour had buzzed, email addresses exchanged and promises of further contact given. As Anne of *Anne of Green Gables* would have said, Clare was of 'the race that knows Joseph'. After only some six minutes of respective digging we unearthed our shared familiarity with the Findhorn Foundation and some of the community members, then skipped on from there to discussions of Greater Plans and Divine Law, life journeys, Iona, rescue helicopters, hospital food, books and Cassie in her role of Good Angel. I also pointed out a large stone built Victorian mansion sitting on the crest of a hill in clear view from the window adjacent to Clare's bed. My cousin has an attic flat in this lovely building which was once a convent and nursing home. From her kitchen window she can see the hospital's helipad which is where the helicopters, bringing sick people in from remote areas of the western islands and highlands, land.

'I always say a little prayer for whoever is in the helicopter,' my cousin has said. 'I just send it out to them. They are someone's mother, sister, brother, child ...'

I told Clare this saying:

'So when you were brought in from Iona you were brought in on a prayer. It's nice to think of that isn't it?'

This of course then lent itself to another twenty minutes on Divine Law. Which is what you talk about in an orthopaedic ward on a Friday night, isn't it?

Not really knowing what to take Clare considering she was leaving the next day, I gave her copy of my last book thinking it might serve to pass an hour or so on her long haul flight, or at least come in useful for bunging at whoever is keeping her awake with their snoring. Clare thanked me for it and said in return that she would retaliate by mailing me a copy of her latest book once she had got home. We said our goodbyes, invited her to stay over with us should she risk another visit to Iona in the future and toddled off home.

A week or so later Kelvin gave me a large packet.

'This came for you yesterday,' he said.

My fingers itched to open it but shop duties demanded other action and I propped it in the staff cupboard. Some twenty minutes later my husband came in with a friend of ours who was visiting from Northern California. Charlie is a Quaker and was en route to lead a Quaker Pilgrimage in the Lake District which is where, apparently, (life is a never ending school), the Quaker movement began. I dug the package out of the cupboard and asked my husband to open it while I got him and Charlie some coffee.

The package contained Clare's book and inside an A4 sheet of typed words entitled 'The Kindness of Strangers'. My husband read what was written there and then silently passed it to me. I noticed there were tears in his eyes.

'I'll read it this evening,' I said, knowing that high emotion and the bookshop don't quite mix.

I may as well not have bothered, for the next minute Charlie was skimming through Clare's letter, pausing, reading aloud, sitting back and swiping his eyes with the back of his hand. It could have been a combination of the malt whisky we had consumed the evening before (we had been demonstrating the tradition of the quaich to our guests), and the physical tiredness from an exerting 48 hour trip to Arran we had all just enjoyed, but somehow I don't think so. No, it was Clare's words of thanks and recognition that there are no accidents in the universe which had the menfolk greetin. That, and the connectedness of all things.

'I live only ten minutes from a hospital,' concluded Clare. 'I'm sure there must be people there who know no-one in Berkeley. You have all been so kind and you have inspired me. When I am recovered and on my feet again, I will 'pass this on', and do for someone else in my local hospital what you have done for me.'

Cloisters, take a pat on the back, I think we done good.

Desmonderata

A boyish looking chap comes to the bookshop at least thrice a week. In response to the fairly common enquiry 'Do you work here?' from a confused customer, he replies 'I'm here all the time' — thus both asserting an undesignated status and usually prompting the enquirer to ask for further assistance. It seems somehow cruel for me to jump in and make clear that Desmond, while rather prevalent in the shop, is nonetheless not a member of staff and I tend to gently intervene without diminishing his self-fashioned standing. Why cruel? Well the bookshop matters to Desmond. Matters greatly. As far as we can judge, coming to the bookshop is a pinnacle of his week's structure. It is what he does. He also goes to the local library to use the computers and, most mornings, to a shopping mall to check out and frequently buy DVDs. It was the search for a particular DVD that first brought him to the shop and, having found a patient bookshop owner, willing to trawl the internet and order various films to Desmond's heart content, he came back again and again and again.

We now expect to see him at some point most days, hurtling in through the door, desperate to off-load to Kelvin his latest requests. If another customer or shop matter has dared to claim Kelvin's attention, he rocks from side to side for a few minutes in the abject hope of saying his piece and if, and only if, he perceives he will need to wait, he sadly wanders over to the table where I am usually pricing books and says '*Hmmm*. How are you?'

I am, you see, not whom he has come to see. I am a useful person to ask where Kelvin is, useful too to say how long he may have to wait until he can see his hero, but in all other things useful to him, I distinctly lack. When in on the shop on my own I don't push other jobs aside and sit at the counter and spend a half hour or so trogging through the buying options and best bargain prices of whatever trilogy or series he is currently keen on. Kelvin has told the staff not to do this, indeed not to let any regular customer monopolise our time. An instruction easier said than done. I have however honed my internet search avoidance skills rather well now and on the first hint of 'Can you just quickly look something up for me?' from Desmond I say 'Yes. But just for a few minutes then I have to get on with jobs Kelvin has left me to do.' This works as Kelvin, in Desmond's books, is God. As such it comes as no surprise to him that the menial staff members should bow to his wishes and respect all his commands.

It is also true that should the staff members spend an hour of their time looking for DVDs we would be denying the mutual pleasure it appears to give Desmond and his hero. For it is not all one-sided. Desmond has his own particular paradigm and operates out of this — a paradigm which other shops would find too demanding to allow. Cloisters however, as you will have gathered by now, runs on slightly different business lines and customers who have, what shall I say … *distinctive?*… behaviourial patterns are viewed by Kelvin as a source of free entertainment. Where members of staff might be heard to mutter slight noises of frustration at the sight of some people presenting themselves and their individual mindset in the shop, Kelvin seems to almost clap his hands and settle in for a long and amusing interlude. There are various regular customers that seem to give him particular good value and Desmond ranks high in this.

Desmond, you see, should not be dismissed lightly. There is more to him than meets the impatient eye. What more? Well, a natural politeness for one. If forced to speak to me while queuing for Kelvin's attention, he will always enquire how I am. The fact that he still has trouble remembering my name after at least a year of visiting the shop is neither here nor there. He has actually helpfully suggested that I change my name to something he can remember. I suggested in return that I could simply be 'The Other One' — a notion which Kelvin also thought quite useful. Desmond then suggested that it would help him in distinguishing me from Serena, a member of staff whom he mentally morfs me with, if I would consider dying my hair. The fact that Serena already has a different hair colour than me doesn't seem to have made any impact. And, the fact that I doubt if he could repeat any single fact I have told him about me, is again neither here nor there. I am simply not on his radar. He is not acting out of rudeness in this but indeed out of honesty. I am not versed in Sci-Fi or Fantasy fiction. I don't like Horror. I am usually too busy to chat more with him than pleasantries. I keep asking him how his hamsters are when he has guinea-pigs. My favourite film is *You've Got Mail*. All of these factors disqualify me from significant import. But even if I did share his fascination with the above genres of films, even if I did get his pet species correct, I still would not be Kelvin and therefore must, by natural law, be demoted in his attentions. He has room for only one deity and that slot has been given to Kelvin. I must accept my lowly place and content myself with quietly listening out for Desmondisms.

It is in the Desmondisms that the special blend which makes up the man is found. He is a benign soul who would like to go placidly in the noise and haste but finds, I suspect, that the noise and haste irritatingly intrudes. And, the more I observe Desmond I see that he is difficult to categorise and slips out of any defining labels. As he hangs over the counter studiously clocking the computer screen as Kelvin scans for titles for him, or as he gets himself a cup of coffee or a 'cold cold drink of water' from the kitchen, or as he answers the questions Kelvin poses him, Desmond often surprises us with a sudden spark of acute observational thought. Watching Kelvin listing a book for an Amazon sale which was judged 'Damaged but still good', Desmond quipped 'Bit like the criminal mind' — a description which had Kelvin doubled up in delighted laughter. Or, when getting in a slight muddle over which DVD Desmond actually wanted to order, Kelvin and I both noted Desmond's intelligent statement, 'Look, let's start with the premise that we'll only order ones in the UK'. A possible product of poor schooling Desmond may be, but his intellect remains 'Damaged but still curiously sharp'. Another instance of this came when I was flicking through a book — Paul Henderson Scott's *Spirits of the Age: Scottish Self Portraits* — which had been ordered by a customer. I was checking the contents as I was curious to know why the customer was keen to order not one but two copies. Running my eye down the list of famous people focused on I noted the name of a contemporary and renowned sculptor whom our town is proud to boast of. The customer who had ordered the book was none other than the famous lad's dad. Just as I had uttered an 'Ah ha!' Desmond trotted into the shop.

'Hallo Desmond, how are you today?'

'Good. Good. What're you reading?'

'Ah, it's quite interesting. This book was ordered by a man whose son has contributed a chapter. And I'm having a wee keek at it.'

'What's the chapter about?'

'It's about his son's life and how he grew to be a celebrated sculptor.'

'And his dad wants to read about that?'

'Yes, I suppose so.'

'Why doesn't he just ask him?'

I paused. Blinked. Pondered. And realised that once again Desmond had homed into a truth which the more complicated of us make complicated.

'Good point,' I said replacing the book back on the Orders shelf, 'Good point.'

We are also thinking of initiating a rather unique shelving classification in the shop thanks to Desmond who told us that he quite liked 'a bit of blood and cleavage'. Jean Plaidy, Nigel Tranter, Georgette Heyer, Stephanie Meyer all spring to mind and that's just for starters. I think it could prove rather attractive to the local customer base.

Furthermore, should Cloisters ever, even in imagination, assemble a quiz team from staff and customer base, I bags Desmond for whatever team I'm in. Provided the questions are about Woody Allen films or Meryl Streep we are home and dry.

Doris

'Hallaw … Hallaw … Are ya there?'

I hear her voice as I come out of the Thriller corridor. Oh Lord Lummy, it's Doris. Of course, it's Monday. It's a Doris day or a 'Doris flypast' as I tend to think of it. I have successfully dodged her visits for a few weeks now by arriving as close to the beginning of my shift as possible, sometimes even lingering at the traffic-lights when I see her bulky form waddle into the shop, and only proceeding when she has waddled out again. Doris tends to appear before our designated opening time of 10.15am in the belief that, as other shops open earlier, we will be too, and it really is only because of the stubborn and obtuse nature of 'that man' that she sometimes finds the bookshop closed. Today though, the lights being on, the storm doors propped open, she gets to come in. And what's more, 'that man' isn't sitting behind the counter. It's her lucky day.

I appear around the Special Illustrator, Wee Books and Notices shelving unit and her face lights up.

'Oh, where've you been? Ah've been coming in 'ere and it's just that stoopid man. He's 'opeless him.

Now, this is part of the strange nature of our bookshop. No matter how qualified, experienced, efficient or helpful any member of staff or the owner himself is, the customers sift though us and decide who is the one they prefer to deal with. Everybody else is just silently, or not so silently, tolerated. Where Desmond adores Kelvin and has trouble remembering my name or purpose, I have been gifted with Doris' affection. Well, having said that, it's a diluted kind of affection, not as simple and direct as Desmond's worship of Kelvin, but more of a workable synergy in that, so far, none of Doris' distinctive way with words has resulted in me dishing the same back. I haven't, as yet, openly opposed her, I appear willing to skoot about the shop looking for her kind of books, will ask her how she is, will complement her on an article of clothing or shoe wear and appear not to notice when she invariably pays 50p short of the price of a book. Try as he might to be pleasant and amiable — which, if Doris only appreciated, is a real decision for Kelvin — he is dismissed as beyond useless.

'He never gets naffing in, that man,' she declares. 'Don't know why he's ere.'

I have tried a few times to explain that as the owner of the establishment, Kelvin does have a role to play in the running of the shop, but I may as well have just nodded and agreed with her for all my reasoning has helped. In her book, 'that man' is beyond redemption and a spurious presence during her visit.

Today she is delighted it is me who is here. And I, having had respite from her for the last three Mondays, have sufficient tolerance in my being to deal with her. I set my mental dial to 'Complicated Elderly Person' mode.

'How are you, Doris?' I ask 'That's a nice colour of raincoat'.

'Yeh, well, don't know what the stoopid weather is doing. Ah 'ate this weather. Stoopid it is. Stoopid. Ah don't bovver. Nawh. Don't bovver. Ah dress to suit myself. Ah got my showts on under it. Look.'

And she hoists up her long lilac raincoat which floats above a bright white pair of trainers, to reveal a pair of wrinkled legs clad in knee-high soft grey socks and a pair of stripy shorts.

I quickly bite my lips then say 'Quite right. Dress how you like. That's best.'

'You bet it is,' she returns. 'Ah don't care what anyone says. Ah dress how ah like. That's what ah say to them. To them stoopid people. Ah only wear ma bra and showts in the house. Don't care. Don't care.'

I try not to picture the possible image. It is too early in the day. I need to pace myself.

'Would you like some coffee?'

'Yeh, and don't make it strong. Keep me up all night you will.'

The fact that there will be no charge for the coffee and the fact that I am willing to break off from whatever else I might have been doing to attend to her needs has no bearing on her psyche or manners. But I expect no less. Best to let her rudeness glide in and out of my consciousness.

I make the coffee and carry it to where she has plonked down on the wicker seat near the door. Doris likes this position. For one it is beside Religion and she has a passionate interest in both Mother Teresa and Pope John Paul II, and it is also right next to the door so she can leave the moment she desires. And there is little point in her roaming around the shop looking at titles for, it seems, that Doris can't or won't read. How she has got thus far in life is therefore rather admirable. Maybe that's where her trigger-happy feisty character takes its impetus from — the determination not to be put down despite what must be an incredible limitation. In Doris' case therefore the maxim that a picture is worth a thousand words is not true. For Doris it is far beyond that — being the text, the whole text and nothing but the text. We know this about her and therefore should a member of staff unearth a large book with lots of pictures, particularly of famous people and events, it is dubbed 'a Doris book' and left in a position ready for her next visit. Doris' dream book would be a large multi-coloured photo collation of her two aforementioned holy gurus off-set with scenes from a hospital (with lots of pics of ward sisters as her favourite aunt was, she has told me, just such a great personage) and, if possible, some gory true crime scenes. To date we have not come across such a volume. So, budding photographers and authors, there's a challenge for you ... and should you take it up you will be assured of at least one delighted customer.

Doris looks at the coffee I have placed next to her.

'Oh my Gawd, that's far too strong. Put more milk in. What d'ya think I am? Ah'll have a fit if ah drink that.'

I take it back, add another two sachets of milk, return it to her, smiling.

'That's a good girl,' she says. 'Did ah tell ya I got a new suite?'

'Oh, how nice. What's it like?'

'Leathah. Blue red leathah. Laffley it is. Laffley. But ah'm not letting that caaw next door sit on it. Naw. Naw way. Fed up with her I am. Fed up. She's not getting her fat ahrse on my new suite. Naw. Naw way.'

Simultaneously wondering what blue-red leather looks like and what kind of existence her neighbour must have, I say placatingly:

'Your place must be looking really nice now. What with your new telly, bed, kitchen and carpets you got recently...'

'Yeh. 'Tis. Nice. Really nice. 'Ere girl ... Get me some books. Naffing rubbish. Naffing from that man. He's useless he is. Useless. Ah'll just sit 'ere a minute.'

Off I trot around the aisles in the fairly pointless quest of finding a book she will like. I have been on holiday recently so maybe, just maybe, something has come in while I was away. And ... Praise be! I spy a book entitled *Famous Faces of the Twentieth Century*. Fantastic. It's large, colourful, and wonder of wonders, has Mother Teresa and JP II in it. I take it triumphantly to Doris.

'Ere. Whas that? Let me see it.'

She plonks her cup down. I make a mental note to wipe up the splodge later and give her the book.

'How much is that? Ah'll buy it. How much is that?'

'It's £3.00.'

'Ere. Ah'll give you £2.50.'

The book is actually priced at £2.50, but having grown accustomed to Doris' trading practices I now add on a 50p when quoting prices. If she were an old biddy who was obviously struggling financially, and if she didn't regularly show me her purchases of silver rings and bracelets, or tell me of her constant new furniture arrivals, I would be tempted to lower the price. As it is however she has unconsciously set up a precedent of this silent game.

She counts out the money then shoves the book into her large blue shopping trolley.

'Ere, get in there you, get in there!'

I wonder if inanimate objects replace people in her life. Her blistering attitude to most living beings must have greatly decreased her social engagements. Books and things can't talk back.

'Right. I'm going home now. Had enuf. Had enuf.'

I've noticed that Doris exits the shop quickly after 'doing me'. I know that she is aware that she (apparently) hasn't given the correct price. She knows she is acting badly but can't somehow stop herself and is getting a thrill from being naughty. But like a child stealing sweeties from the Pick n Mix, once they are stuffed in a pocket, her usual strategy is to leave and leave quickly, her four milk-sacheted coffee only half drunk.

She hoists herself up, smooths her raincoat down, picks up her copious walking stick, hangs it from the back collar of her coat (yes, really), grabs her trolley and manoeuvres herself towards the door. As she trundles over the doorway she turns back and, responding to some impulse from her higher self, says:

'You're a nice girl. Ah'll treat you to a meal sometime. Ah'll do that. Ah'll treat ya. Yeh, I will.'

My heart goes on high alert, my mind darts forward into the possible scene, shudders and retreats, but I calmly say:

'That's kind, but my day tends to be pretty full up.'

'That's awlright. The place ah go opens at nine o'clock in the mawning. They do me a nice breakfast, they do — fish n chips, peas n ice-cream. We'll go there. Yeh. See ya then.'

And off she goes, leaving me planning how to be incredibly busy for the next decade.

Autodídaktos

Ed is the prime example of why it is utterly stupid to presume that the working class aren't interested in, or capable of, deep erudition. He's a retired ship-yard blacksmith who has spent his adult life reading, thinking, learning and reading some more. Ed, unconsciously and entirely naturally, follows the tradition of the Radical weavers in our town who were both workers, poets and political activists. Had his life been different, had he had the opportunity — which basically means had there been money in his family — he would have gone to university, no doubt excelled and spent his life in academia. As it was he slugged it out in heavy industry, reading what he could, when he could, talking with people, seeking out those who wanted to talk about the things he considered mattered, thirsting for knowledge of how the world worked and what the great minds were thinking. He is a living testament to the intelligence of the aspiring working class whom many far poorer-read government ministers, focused on the well-off members of society, don't believe exist.

Ed's favourite subjects for discussion are Wittgenstein, Marx, Lenin, Trade Unionism, Western film, Ezra Pound, the media, jazz, Machiavelli and how stupid the Tories are. On discovering that I knew a smidgeon about Literary Theory, he now flings me nuggets of thought to do with the differences between New Criticism and Postmodernism or the thinking behind Vladimir Propp's morphology of the folktale. He is fascinated by the rules and classifications of poetry and basically continually causes me to scour the depths of my memory when cobbling up an answer for him. He studiously reads *The Guardian*, the arts section of *The Financial Times* and enjoys the main section of *The Observer* once I have finished with it. Ed is also the only person I have come across who immediately recognised the literary allusion embedded in the first line of my last book.

His knowledge is rough, rudimentary at times and he has the slightly frantic feeling to his search for sound knowledge. He is often unsure of how to pronounce foreign sounding names having never heard them spoken aloud and despairs a little that he will ever catch up. What point exactly he is catching up to is unanswerable. Do any of us know how it all connects? Do any of us in our life journey believe we understand it all? And if we profess to know, it is certain we don't. But Ed goes on reading, reading, sifting, making notes – 'I have three pens, one black for notes that I have copied from books, one green for my questions, one red for where I disagree,' — oh, would that all students were so assiduous in their learning. Just as Ed would study a complex welding problem, work out a plan before he reached for his tools, he similarly studies a text, tracing its contours, its margins, its paradigm, checking how it fits to others, notes where it is weak, records its nature and then moves on to where it is leading his reading.

His favourite poems are 'The Leveller' by Robert Graves, 'The Raven' by Edgar Allan Poe, 'Hugh Selwyn Mauberley' by Ezra Pound – none of which I am familiar with — and anything by Pablo Neruda whom, Ed unconsciously echoing Edwin Morgan, says, 'can write poetry about anything'.

His intellect, had there only been that missing opportunity, would have been honed and shaped by immersion in university-led scholarship and discourse. But it is passionate, and at 76 years of age, that is quite wonderful. There are many university teachers who, knowing no other kind of life, are divorced from the vital essence of their specialist field, who see it as a job, a means towards easy retirement, rather than a privileged propitious way of being. They could do with a few sessions with Ed to test what they really know.

Ed was ill last winter. Pneumonia snuck up on him as he continued to try to do his daily routine. He lost weight, lost energy, lost a lot of his hearing, ended up in hospital where he later told us he 'had no complaints'. Solid working-class stock, the last thing Ed will ever do is criticise tired, over-stretched and understaffed ward nurses. His family worried about him. His beloved little grand-daughter, Megan, took to holding his hand while crossing the street so he wouldn't fall.

'I'm no goin' tae die yit, I telt them,' he said 'I've git too much reading tae dae.'

He reminds me of my dear old dad at times. Dad had the same need to present himself as respectable despite growing up in an east end of Glasgow tenement, despite having to leave school at fourteen, despite having no academic qualification to his name. Ed, like my Dad would have done had he been alive today, comes to the bookshop shaved and clothed smartly, shirt and tie, pressed trousers, jacket, raincoat, brushed shoes, eight-piece cap. The only sartorial difference between Ed and my Dad is the walking stick and the shoulder bag slung across Ed's shoulders necessary for his newspapers, various articles he has had downloaded from the library and the books he has ordered from the shop.

A quirky turn of phrase delights and amuses him. Once, when I was describing a literary character, who was bisexual, and said 'He kicks with both feet,' Ed laughed and laughed and went off repeating it to himself. The labyrinthine world of the internet has recently been opened up to him as he has, with fairly little tuition, become familiar with how to use a computer. Before coming to the bookshop he will book a two hour session at his local library where he finds words after words after words to stimulate his thoughts and print off at an alarming rate.

He loves to come in and talk about what was in Saturday's *Guardian Review*. Busy with other happenings I sometimes find myself quickly scanning it early on a Monday morning before coming to work as I know he will quiz me on it and be disappointed if I haven't read it and therefore have no comment to make. Why I don't spend my weekends reading all that I could read remains a mystery to him. Perhaps, one fantastical day, when I am able to employ a cook, cleaner and gardener I may edge near to matching Ed's consumption of the written word. But that's probably doubtful.

Bakhtin's theory of the carnival has recently drawn his attention. He asked me about it. My mind had to reach back into the depths of my memory and the huge tangle of thought that is literary theory. All I could contribute was the example of how Shakespeare used the idea of suspension of the usual in his decision to have Juliet and Romeo meet at a masked ball — and thanked my lucky stars that I had recently read the play as part of my other life as a tutor of Higher English. But exactly what Bakhtin argued had long flown from my memory box. I looked it up when I got home and discovered that he perceived the carnival to offer four categories — i.e. free interaction between people who would not normally meet; eccentric behaviour; opportunity for misalliance or crossing of boundaries; free expression. This all sounds rather too familiar to me. Was Mr Bakhtin, I wonder, a frequenter of his local bookshop?

One of Ed's latest fields of study is Florentine politics. Apart from the almost unreadable *Romola* by George Eliot, which I have never managed to struggle through, I can't say that I have given much of my life to this discourse. What is wonderful about Cloisters however is that we very often don't need our own knowledge to meet the conversation or subject needs of customers. One morning, having settled himself with his black coffee with three sugars and a wee drop of cold water to make it drinkable, Ed said that he was continuing to enjoy reading of 14th century Florentine goings on. I suddenly remembered Kelvin asking me about a book, required by another customer, which I was hopelessly searching the very dusty part of my memory to tell Ed about.

'It was on that powerful Italian family, the um … you know … the … um …'

'Medicis,' called a woman's voice from Children.

'Yes! Those chaps.' I said. 'Thanks.'

'Oh, ho,' called Ed to the unseen voice. 'How do you know about them?'

A head appeared around the corner.

'I've a PhD in early history,' it said.

I recognised Mairi-Anna, a fairly new customer to Cloisters whom I've already enjoyed talking Scottish politics with. Today she is in with her daughter who is having fun choosing books as part of her birthday spoils. Thus, blessing the bookshop gods who have once again provided the perfect person for a specialised topic, I left them both to chew over the ins and outs of the royal house and political dynasty that was clan Medici. I was, thankfully, redundant.

His impressive knowledge notwithstanding, Ed has, to his credit, not abandoned the courtesy of admitting if he is wrong. When the Orange Walk came up in conversation — there is a Lodge just round the corner from the bookshop which treats us to the usual bizarre marching spectacle every July — I said that it amazed me how Scots could be loyal to such a creed as it was William of Orange who had signed the order for the Massacre of Glencoe.

'Why don't people read a history book?' I had chuntered.

Ed looked puzzled and then said that he thought I had the wrong king as William of Orange wasn't on the throne at the time of the massacre.

This effectively stopped me in my flow. I had been arguing that for a long time. I tried to remember the date of the massacre. That was hazy. I tried to bring to mind the dates of William of Orange. That was more than hazy. Hmmm. Not on such firm ground as I thought I was.

I meant to look it up. I have any amount of books at home that would verify or falsify my argument. There are books in the shop that would do that too. But of course I didn't. Other things happen at home that eclipse intentions I make in the shop.

Ed, however, true scholar that he is, did do the research. A few days later he presented himself at the counter.

'I've an apology to make to you,' he said looking me straight in the eye.

'Me? Really? What for?'

'You were right and I was wrong. William of Orange was on the throne at the massacre of Glencoe in 1692. And I said to myself 'you need to go and apologise to that lassie'. So here I am.'

The root of the word 'humility' is the Latin 'humilitas' i.e. 'of the ground' — a quality which has little to do with self abnegation or deprecation. It is instead about the attempt to be clear-sighted. To reach out for truth. And to be strong enough to admit when you're wrong. Would that other more famous minds remembered that. Sometimes it takes an unpretentious working-class scholar to remind us of the actual root of things.

Maud

She tends to come in quietly with a quizzical smile on her intelligent face which is normally a little flushed from the rapid walk — one of many she will do, without thinking, every day as buses, taxis or ownership of a car is just plain silly to her thinking when two strong legs do nicely. She tends to have a large reusable strong plastic bag hanging heavily from her arm which is stuffed full of books, papers, and knitting — all vital equipment for her campaign to save the world by yesterday. Committed environmentalist. Committed carer for the world and its inhabitants. When I see Maud the final line from Lewis Grassic Gibbon's *Sunset Song* flits through my mind as she, most certainly, possesses 'a lamp quiet-lighted and kind in [her] heart'. A soul only need mildly suggest that it needs help and she's there. Putting a wild garden to rights, patiently explaining the whys and wherefores of the English language to young offenders doing time in prison, adapting a complicated knitting pattern (of her own design) for someone looking for a birthday present, offering a meal or a walk for a bereaved spirit, spending copious hours trawling through on or offline Scottish records for purposes of a family research project or helping friends with the lambing, are but some of her pursuits. Wide and varied in her interests Maud will never be bored — she simply hasn't the time. When she landed a job on the other side of the country, to which she travels by public transport every day, Kelvin suggested to her that she drop some of her normal altruistic occupations. 'I can't do that,' was her answer. She could do that. Of course she could, but she won't while there is breath in her body. There is just far too much need and someone just has to get on and do it.

There are many sections of the bookshop that grab her attention — although I can't say I have ever seen her wander around the vault of Sci-Fi, Crime, Horror and Fantasy. She prefers History, Scottish Non-Fiction, Children or maps and postcards, and will often pull out a book with a delighted exclamation and then proceed to tell me of the writer, of the illustrator, of the type-script, of other editions and of the publisher. And I have to admit there are many times when the information is completely new to me. She will then collect a bundle of books, sighing as she does so because they will undoubtedly bust her closely controlled budget while yet delighting her inner being.

The physical outcome of this desire to fix the world is a slight tendency to talk, rapidly, with barely a pause for breath, about everything that is in her mind. With all its threads twisting and turning and jumping over each other in an effort to describe all that she has been involved with since we last met, conversation with Maud is rather like listening to the most intricate Shetland knitting design chatting to itself. Strangely enough I don't find this annoying. There is just such goodness in her that to interject and attempt to bring her fountain of talk to a standstill, would be like dousing a shining light leaving us in silent but miserable dark.

And I admire all that she does. Particularly her decision to not create waste or at least to create as little as possible. I often think of this as I am, once again, emptying another assortment of plastic, glass and paper into our recycling bin. Yes, it will be recycled, that's a good thing, but wouldn't it be better if so much of our food didn't come in just so much packaging? And the energies and materials used to make all that packaging were used for something else? Wouldn't it be both good for our planet and our aesthetics if we could revert back to those great deli-type food stores where so much of the produce is unpackaged, freshly cut, shored and weighed to our individual desires? Where items were wrapped in brown paper, hessian or cotton bags or put straight into your own personal shopping bag? And wouldn't it be good if these weren't just found in posh suburbs but were the norm everywhere? If Maud were in charge they would be.

She also thinks about how we continually squander the earth's resources by turning up the dial in our over-heated cars, houses, places of work and of leisure instead of pulling on a warm jumper or coat. I have to admit though that her practice of not having the central heating on unless visitors are coming — and crawling underneath a pile of home-made blankets and shawls so to listen to the radio on a cold winter evening — is too much for my wimpish spirit. This reminds me too much of growing up in my childhood home pre the instalment of central heating, seeing ice form hard around the inside of our bedroom window, having to run over patches of freezing linoleum, which tore at my chronically cold feet, to reach the comfort of the two-bar electric fire in the living room, so to get dressed for school. I'm all for thoughtful environmental practices but my bones are not always in agreement. But, as it was in my childhood and was for Maud when I first met her, such measures were not a chosen philosophy but necessary strictures if she was simply to survive. I suspect though that now, even though she is now earning, her heating is still resolutely turned off and the money saved spent on books that fuel her kaleidoscope of passionate pursuits. We have need of the Mauds of this world, they remind us that we can do life differently, more authentically, more ethically, and because of them we may just have a world to keep living in.

One of my best times with Maud was on Christmas Eve a couple of years back. I hadn't wanted to work that day, I had too much to do at home but if you work in retail then tradition demands that shops are open on this precious day. It was with a slightly sluggish heart that I was staffing the shop on my own. The shop was busy though and there was a tangible feeling of excitement in the air, and there is, it has to be said, something rather Dickensian about being in a second-hand bookshop on that day of the year. Many customers were still searching for that distinctive present for a beloved one, some just wanted to be somewhere that wasn't punting out tired Christmas hit songs that had been bombarding shoppers since early November. Customers told me of their festive plans, some told me of the lack of them, some told me of their views on Christmas, some were happy and some were melancholy.

Maud appeared in the shop around mid-morning. She didn't seem too bothered about doing her usual skim around the shelves but instead produced a small tin wherein was some of her homemade fruit cake. At this juncture in her life Maud didn't have a paid job and was living on her wits and ingenuity. Her thoughtfulness of making cake and bringing it to share in the shop was the stuff of widow's mite and was more welcome than any expensive present. As it now felt like hours since my early breakfast, proffered cake was most tempting. I promptly made some tea but, instead of taking it to the table which was peopled by browsing customers weighing up if this book would be the right thing for Uncle Charlie, Aunt Susan or wee Jimmy, I took the steaming cups into the staff corridor. The staff corridor is strictly off-limits for customers. Now and again we get a wide ranging browser who either fails to notice the sign outlining 'Sorry, Staff Only!' or pretends they can't read and who wanders down it and has to be shooed out. The books in the staff corridor are complicated — some are awaiting sorting, some are awaiting Amazon listing, some are overflow copies of volumes already in the shop, some are the results of special orders, some are just sheer homeless loiterers which we can't be bothered dealing with. Only the staff understand the classifications at work there. Actually that's not true, it is perhaps only Kelvin that knows, mostly, what is going on there and even he is often heard to exclaim 'What is that!? How did they get there?'

But the shop was busy and there wasn't enough cake for everyone. Maud looked tired. She wasn't going to start pulling books off shelves and wreaking havoc. I made the executive decision to dust off a set of ancient old encyclopaedias, bound for the Make Us An Offer window, and tell her to sit on them (another major 'No No' in the shop). I then closed up one of the large boxes full of books to be recycled and sat myself on it. Out of the line of fire from other customers we chinked our tea cups together and wished each other 'Happy Christmas!' Maud passed me a generous slice of her yummy cake and we both slurped and munched our festive feast. I was suddenly content to be where I had to be.

Studied Criminality

'This is a stick-up!'

I look up from the Amazon inventory. See a man in the doorway and shriek:

'That's rubbish! Do it again with more aggression. It won't work otherwise!'

He goes back out. Waits a second. Batters in with more force. This time he is waving something in front of him.

'Bit better,' I say 'Whit's that you've got there?'

'It's my 'gun'?'

'Mmmm. Not sure. I mean, what's it going to do? Flash a light in my face?'

'Aye, well, worth a try,' he says and drops his mobile phone into his jacket pocket.

'And I think you should leave the big bag at home next time, it's dead weight.'

'But I thought I might need it for The Swag?'

'No. You almost got it caught in the door. Or could have tripped over it and that isn't cool. Anyway the amount of cash you'd get here could go in your shirt pocket.'

'Point taken,' he says affably. 'Anyhoo. Where's the big man? Out skiving leaving you tae deal with masked robbers?'

'A mask. That could improve your act. Remember that next time.'

'Good thinking.'

'Are you wanting to order a book? Now that the stick-up didn't get you anywhere?'

'Aye. May as well. I'll pass the time. Can I have a coffee?'

'Sure thing. And what's the title of the book? I'll do a wee internet search while we're waiting for the boss.'

'Eh, I think it's *Gangsters from the Ghetto*.

'Ah. Homework.' I say punching the keyboard. 'Mind you read it properly.'

Real War

'Have you any war books?'

'Lots.'

'Not old war.'

'Such as the wars of Independence, Roses or American Civil?

'Not any of that.'

'WWI or II ?'

'No. Not them.'

'So ... modern day war? Cold War? Gulf War?'

'No, not them either.'

'Em ...'

'War with Orcs.'

'Ah, the Tolkien section is just over there sir.'

Genres

The first customer of the day — a velvet clad, thin, long raven-haired man — asks if we have any books by Crowley. Who? Do a rapid Google search and learn that he is the late Victorian occultist and founder of the Thelemite philosophy. Judging by his pic on Wikipedia he looks a rather intense chap. So does this customer, who also looks incredibly like Mike Scott of *The Waterboys*. I do a double check to make sure it really is not him. No, wrong voice and he is a different shape. But I wonder if he has modelled himself on Mr Scott as they certainly share a passion for esoteric stuff. This customer will be happy at Paranormal and I point him to the section. He appears back at the counter some fifteen minutes later with Frazer's *The Golden Bough* in hand. We chat a bit about the need for humans to find an underlying unifying text. He says he will take Frazer's monumental study on holiday with him. I ask where he's going. He looks a little uncomfortable. I wait for him to say something like 'a Wicca festival' or some other gathering exploring the dark arts. 'Majorca,' he says 'and please don't judge me.'

Eight minutes later. An overweight, trainspotter type appears. His tummy is bursting out of his over-stretched kagoul. Too many hot pies at the end of chilly platforms I suppose. Buys *A Guide to the Steam Railways of Great Britain* edited by Chris Cook and none other than the Rev W Awdry — inventor of the Fat Controller and those troublesome trucks. My mind is suddenly full of Ringo Star narrating the seemingly endless BBC adaptions of *Thomas the Tank Engine* and my pre-school son learning colours through the medium of Rev Awdry's characters — hence red becoming 'the James one' and green renamed as 'the Henry one' etc. We still have Sam's collection of 'Thomas' trains' safely boxed somewhere waiting for another generation of wee hands fascinated by them. I suspect the local auction room folk would be interested in them, but we ain't selling. The only real steam train I have first hand experience of is what is now dubbed 'The Harry Potter line' — or the Fort William to Mallaig line. My great aunt lived in Arisaig and, as a child, long before the days of J K Rowling's imagination, we travelled perhaps once a year, up from Glasgow, to stay with the Fort William great aunt, then got on the Mallaig train the next morning and chuffed down to Arisaig where Great Aunt Mary would have tea and criticism waiting for us in her wee flat above the library. I could tell the customer all of these memories, but don't — suspecting it is wiser to simply smile, take the money, give the change, put the book in a bag and say good-bye. This chap looks ready to offload his accumulated knowledge built up over the years on any suspecting person and I would prefer that wasn't me.

The window-cleaner is next up. Having swarmed over our large windows he comes in to claim his wages. I give him the requisite £6. I muse on what he thinks of the shop. Is he at all curious as to what we sell in here? Does reading have any place in his life? Are we just a place that needs its windaes washin?

My reverie is interrupted by the appearance of a small dumpy looking woman who looks as if she has been taking care of people all her life. The type of woman who will reach out and touch or hold your arm when talking. Unconsciously adding comfort and reassurance. She wants to know if we have *Call the Midwife* by Jennifer Worth. Oh, yes, that's on the telly isn't it? I search my mind. It could be in what Kelvin likes to call 'Women's Writing'. I haven't yet summoned the energy to argue that one out, but I do wonder what intelligent women writers, from the time of Mary Wollstonecraft to Germaine Greer, might make of the classification. I prefer to silently borrow George Eliot's coinage of 'Silly Women Novelists' or the less contentious 'Romance Writing' for this section. We go up to the section and search there. No joy. I quickly scan mainstream Fiction. No joy either. New Books. Nope. I return to the till to take a note of the customer's name and phone number so to keep her informed if the book comes in. She puts her bag down and, as she does so, her eye falls on three small shelves of books opposite the counter. They all have white spines and backgrounds with front covers depicting faces of young children looking scared or traumatised. The staff have dubbed these the 'Sad Books.'

'Here it is!' she exclaims.

And so it is.

'Oh, it's a Sad Book,' I say without thinking.

'Well. Maybe bits. But my pal says it's great. I thought it wid be sittin wi these kind of books.'

'I think you should work here instead of me,' I say.

She smiles. 'Aye, well, maybe once the grandkids and are aff ma hands. But ah'll enjoy a guid read afore they come in frae the school. Thanks hen.'

She potters out, carrying her large bags of shopping.

A chap who has been hovering around Poetry then comes over to me.

'Scuse me, do you have any poetry of C J Dennis?'

'Eh, I'm sorry, but I don't actually know who that is.'

'Oh, he was the cousin of Robert Service. He was Australian.'

'Service I do know and we keep him here,' I say showing him the upper shelves of Scottish Fiction.

Memories of my dad reciting 'The Cremation of Sam McGee' swim up in my mind. And us children groaning 'Oh no, not again!' but delighting in the story and especially the line 'I stuffed in Sam McGee,' because Dad always did a brilliant imitation of the action at his point.

'But C J Dennis, I'm afraid you'll probably have to look through anthologies for.'

'I want to read some because my brother in Australia likes him and we could discuss it next time we Skype each other. It's good to have something prepared or you end up talking about the weather and other stupid things.'

'Good point,' I say, mentally admiring his diligence.

A half hour later — the Dennis chap gone without his desired poet but having bought one of Service's books — an elderly chap brings three old skiing books to the counter. I hate skiing. I am absolutely rubbish at it. I have however taken lessons sufficient so that should someone I deeply cared about need me to ski, to save their life, I would *probably* be able to do it. I am good at stopping though — mainly because I don't actually get going in the first place. I think about telling this to the customer as I look at the covers of the books.

'Quality, aren't they?' he says.

'Yes, they're certainly interesting,' I reply. The covers make me think of 1950s knitting patterns for roll neck sweaters and balaclavas shown off by male models who are laughing and pointing into the distance.

'I've skied for over forty years,' he says.

'And do you still do it?' I ask expecting him to demur.

'Oh, yes, I'm going to die with my skis on,' he grins.

'That'll be a good exit,' I say.

'And when I can't ski, like today, because I'm here and there's no snow, I just like to read about it.'

I think about a mature student I once taught who told me that when she couldn't sleep she would get out a map, trace the contours with her finger and imagine what the terrain was like, how long it would take her to walk from a to b, what clothing she might wear, what she'd have in her backpack, who she'd like to walk with, what time of year would be best. She would then find that her agitated mind had become quietened by this contemplative exercise and she'd climb back into bed and fall into a deep doze dreaming of grassy trails, cool breezes and mountain-top views. Occasionally I do something similar with my garden when sleep eludes me. I imagine it as an empty space, surrounded by solid old red brick walls, a flowering apple tree in the corner, an old bench in another, an archway covered with healthy honey-suckle and interweaving clematis in the other, two or three raised beds rising above slate pathways, the soil dark and rich, waiting for planting … If I am honest though this can have the effect not of deep and peaceful slumber but of despair at what is actually going on in my existing garden. I usually end up hauling myself out of bed and going in search of camomile tea and a banana. And I think any attempt to utilise an imaginative contemplation of the joys of ski-ing down a glassy precipice would leave me with serious palpitations instead of restful sleep. Best therefore again to smile and simply say to this ski-ing aficionado that I hope he enjoys his chosen books.

The shop then goes quiet and I get on with weeding out the Pre-Seventeenth Century shelf.

Just before noon a dad comes in carrying a pink toddler. The dad goes into the Thriller corridor with the toddler. I hear the toddler come out, bored already by fast car chases and men with egos. She makes her way past the table and into Children. Amazing. It's either previous knowledge or some intrinsic draw to a subject area she understands. She plonks herself down on the floor. Levers a large shiny book out of one of the Pre-School boxes beside her, opens the book and pointing her wee chubby finger at the words proceeds to tell herself a story which seems to compose of a random string of words being repeated over and over again. She's quite happy though and conscientiously turns and flattens the pages as she goes. A born reader at work. The dad comes out of Thrillers, goes over to his daughter, and asks:

'Will we get you that book? Would you like it?'

She shakes her wee head. Puts the book as best she can back in the plastic tub, picks another out that is the same shape and size and gives it to her dad.

'Oh, you've read the other one already have you?' he says, 'Ok, we'll get this one. C'mon then.'

They bring *Kipper's Toybox*, by the wonderful Mick Inkpen, over to the counter.

'Smart cookie, your wee girl,' I say.

'Aye,' he beams. 'Dead smart. She loves books already. Spends ages telling herself stories out of them. She'll get a surprise when she learns to read what's actually written in them. But I don't know if she'll have as much fun.'

'Sounds like you've a writer in the making there.'

'Aye. Mibby that's it. Never thought of that. Mibby I should be teaching her to write.'

'Yes. I think you should,' I laugh and watch them go. The wee girl clutching her shiny book.

And so it goes on. People trickle in every ten to fifteen minutes. All with their own agenda — some already knowing what they want to search for, others emphatically 'Just Browsing' or Just Curious. Around 1pm a young schoolgirl comes in. She's been in before and I think is the daughter of the chap who owns the Chinese restaurant next door. She's always impeccably turned out — even today, a school holiday when most young folk are loafing around in their skinny jeans, Converses and baggy sweatshirts or cardigans, this lass has on polished shoes, black tights, black skirt, a neat pink blouse and a smart black cardigan. She may, of course, be helping her dad in the restaurant and would prefer more sloppy gear, but somehow I don't think so. Neatness is in her nature. She asks me, quietly and very politely, if she could see a copy of *The Diary of a Wimpy Kid, Book One,* by Jeff Kinney. Huzzah! My marketing strategy has paid off. I deliberately placed this book in the window to attract passers-by. Kinney's books are a great favourite with the younger readers and disappear off the shelf usually within an hour or so of being placed there. This time I think it may be a record — the copy this young lass wants was put there around fifteen minutes prior to her passing. She pays me the money and goes off clutching the book close to her. I hope she gets a long enough tea-break this afternoon to allow her to plunge into it.

The demure Chinese lass is followed by a family or rather what appears to be an extended family, all enjoying each other's company. There are both West of Scotland and southern English accents being bandied about. Ah, one branch visiting the other. They are a lively crew and spend a few moments exclaiming about the shop. The Scottish contingent are apparently proud of it and the English lot compare it favourably to one in their own town. It doesn't matter that I can't remember seeing the Scottish family in here before as it's just nice that they feel they can boast about the literary prowess of our shop. Perhaps putting me to the test, one of the young girls, who looks around nine years of age, asks if we have any books on ballet. My mind shoots to 'the Wells books' which I loved many many years ago, despite the fact that I did Highland dancing while wishing I could do the more brazen tap or elegant ballet classes and despite the fact that my social environ was very very different from that depicted in Lorna Hill's books.

I look at the young lass.

'You look like a ballet dancer,' I say 'Are you?'

'Yes,' she says extending her arms upwards in an elegant arc, 'I am, at least … I take lessons.'

'And I take it that you have already read *Ballet Shoes*? Or 'the Wells books?'

'Um. No. No, I haven't. What are they?'

Ah. Enthusiastic dancer she may be but her literary muscles need some exercise. Or, perhaps that's a little harsh. After all, I read these books when I was her age, and in her eyes that means they were written in the dark ages. But a ballerina is a ballerina, the magic of the image is surely common to all ages. So I point Noel Streatfeild's novel out to her. And I am Meg Ryan in that scene in *You've Got Mail* where, having closed the door of her lovely independent bookshop for children — *The Shop Around The Corner* — for the last time, having been roller-coasted out of business by the huge Fox Books, (aka Borders?), who set up around the corner from her, is tearfully exploring just what it is that the global chain has that she didn't. And of course we, as viewers, see that while Fox Books may have discounts and coffee and couches, the staff are woefully lacking as to knowledge of a timeless classic in children's literature. Meg, or rather her character Kathleen Kelly, overhears a customer ask a young sales assistant if they have 'the shoe books'. This means nothing to him, whereas to Kathleen it means the famous series by Noel Streatfeild. She intervenes and points the assistant and customer in the right direction thus simply demonstrating that there are some areas of expertise you just don't get from 'in-store training' or from a slick MBA. Nope. For that you just have to be a reader all your life.

So I show the young girl the Streatfeild books.

'Oh, these look good,' she says 'but do you have any real ballerinas?'

I want to quip that they are all on their lunch break, but seeing the seriousness in her face, I hold back and instead show her the shelves in Theatre which have books on famous personages of Sadler's Wells and such like. We find a large A4 book, with black and white photographs depicting Fonteyn and Nureyev at their peak of perfection. I leave the young lass on the wicker seat next to the door, slowly turning the pages, totally entranced. The shop doesn't exist for her anymore. She's in the front stalls … the orchestra is playing … the dancers are dancing … enchantment surrounds her.

Crowley to Fonteyn in under four hours. Wonder where the rest of the day will take me?

Favourite Things

Kindness, no matter what the stupid tabloids tell us, is not dead. Over the last few years working in the bookshop when I have done little more than smile, ask if help is required, direct to an appropriate shelf, serve coffee or tea, tot up a price for someone selling books, advise on worth of a book and blether, blether and blether, all of which I am paid to do (well, maybe not the blethering), I find myself in receipt of unmerited kindness. This kindness comes in various forms.

A butternut squash from a chap who is piling up a stash of books to pay for at a future date.

A copy of Fauré's 'Dolly Suite' (better known as 'the Listen With Mother music'), from a customer who had patiently trolled through our boxes of piano music in a futile search of same and, with whom, I had enjoyed a good natter about learning the piano.

An assortment of enticing biscuits from regular and not so regular customers who have noted our fondness for them (biscuits that is).

A pint of unpasteurised goat's milk from Slovakia — from Marek's father who once farmed the same and which, when added to my husband's usual recipe, made amazingly air-light fluffy bread.

A psuedo-silver ring from Doris — but as I wisely kept it in the staff cupboard for when she asked for it back, which she did the next day, I don't think this really counts.

A stylish scarf from a customer who was cleaning out her wardrobe and who had noted that I usually have one around my neck.

A live demonstration of the workings of a folding bike as I had mentioned I was thinking of buying one — this from a chap who styles himself a 'gardinot' (which is apparently distinct from a guerrilla gardener) — and who further offered to watch the shop while I went for a wee shot on it. Could only imagine Kelvin's response had I done this.

Copies of poems or passages from a book — often results of an interesting blether with 'Alan History' or 'The Kirkie Museum man'.

And, perhaps the most bizarre — four tracts in a sealed envelope explaining the Orange Order. Am not quite sure what prompted this, but there you go. Maybe they had got word of what I said about the Massacre of Glencoe and thought to persuade me of their side of events.

Random Finds

Hardly a day that goes by without someone wanting to either give or sell us some books. There are some set reasons for them wanting to do this which are normally located in the following reasons:

They are moving house.

They need to clear space on their shelves.

An elderly relative has died and they are clearing their house.

A son or daughter has left home and they are clearing their room.

They've read all their books and want cash to buy more.

They've bought a Kindle.

They have finished their course of study and never ever want to see the books again.

They are finished with some loved books but want them to go 'to a good home'.

The books are remnants of a charity bookstall.

They've had the books a long time and, having watched too many episodes of 'Flog It', believe they are immensely valuable and want us to pay them lots of money.

Each person then has a slightly different relationship to their books but the bottom line is that, regardless of their reasons for bringing us the books, they are at the point of wanting to let go of them. Well, that's true mostly. Sometimes after we have priced a book, leafed through it a little, noted the date, the condition, perhaps even the obscurity of it, the customer will then suddenly say 'You know, I might keep that one. It was my dad's/ mum's/ grannie's/ I remember them reading it.' On hearing this we promptly hand it back. We have more than enough books without taking any that don't want to come to us. To us, it is a book, a sellable item, even if curious or unusual. For us it has no treasured memory. But the link between the person selling and us isn't quite severed because of what can linger in a book.

Things found in books are like glimpses or, as the Scots better puts it, glisks of something that have been caught in time's web, ousted from the context that would fully explain. With each one comes questions, shades of dimmed voices, scenes, memories all beyond our grasp. We know nothing about them for certain, we can only surmise, make up, fantasise. Or perhaps just hold for a moment and wonder. Things found in books are time-travellers, divorced from their origins while retaining a remnant of them, in all possibility never to return. Being human though, and therefore, like seals and Hobbits, naturally curious, we like to jalouse something of the previous owner or owners. We amuse ourselves by making stabs at guessing the interests, travels, thoughts, celebrations, relationships and values of former readers.

Take, for example, a 1957 hardback edition of Christabel Bielenberg's autobiography *The Past is Myself* which I unearthed from a box of books recently sold to us. At home we already have a paperback copy of her account of life in Germany under the horrors of Nazism. It was given to my husband one Christmas by his Irish god-father, Christopher, who recognised that arguments between countries can never be neatly divided into which is right and which wrong. Inside the argument, struggling for sheer survival, are people, ordinary people such as English-born Christabel and her German husband Peter, trying to keep a sense of integrity, morality and love, despite the atrocious attitudes and decrees of higher authorities. It is a tale which my husband's maternal side of the family understand. My mother-in-law, Dorothy, is half German, half Irish. Prior to the outbreak of WWII, her Irish father joined the British army and was sent to Egypt. Not believing that war would break out, her German mother went from the army accommodation in Aldershot, England, with her two children and expected unborn baby, to visit her parents in Hindenburg. Their planned return to England was delayed and delayed again due to a series of events — the death of the grandfather, the arrival of the new baby brother then the serious illness of Dorothy's younger sister. War broke out and the family were trapped. Dorothy wrote of this experience in an article 'A Childhood in Germany' published in her college journal, *Postscript*, in 1952 :

> So there we were in Germany, looked on as enemies. We lived in a big town called Hindenburg, right on the Polish border. Most of our German friends left us, only a few old school friends of Mammy's remained. I could not understand why children were not allowed to play with me. Even in Kindergarten I was not able to remain long. Our nurse-maid would not stay with us because she insisted we were an English household, although the house belonged to my grandmother. We remained in Hindenburg until it got so bad that the police said they could not protect us any longer, and it would be advisable to go to another place where we were not known. We left Hindenburg in 1942.

Reaching the safe harbour of an uncle's rented chateau in the village of Tuntchendorf in the Glatzer mountains, in what is now Poland, the little family stayed there some years, happy despite the increasing hardships of shortage of food.

> We got only half the rations the Germans got. [...] Mammy went out nearly every night to some farm to get anything she

could on the Black Market, everything was so dear. She often
had to pay a shilling for one egg.

Finally Tuntchendorf became too unsafe as the Russians started to move eastwards and Dorothy, with her mother and two siblings, left in January 1945. Travelling initially by train and then by lorry, they made a nightmarish journey across war-torn Europe.

One evening we entered Pilsen. It was a terrible sight, the
bombers had just left, the houses were still burning, the mountain
was still glowing. I was afraid they might return. From there
we travelled through Klatten and Prague on to Eisentein on the
Czechoslovakian border. Here we slept during the night in a
waiting room where people lay huddled on the floor, and I was so
tired I just put my head on my arms and went to sleep. Mammy
tried to find lodgings for us. It was February and bitterly cold.

In Frankfurt-am-Main they lived in a house once owned by Jews and survived on *'flour soup and ate dry bread'*. Finally, one miraculous night Dorothy was woken by her mother telling her their father had come for them — the Red Cross having managed to link up the family. In the comparative safer transport of an army lorry they travelled through Aachen and into Belgium where they lived for a few months, until finally going by train to the coast of France, by ship to England and eventually home to Cork, Ireland.

Because of this family story, I had always meant to read Bielenberg's account of her own experiences, but hadn't done so. When the edition, published by Chatto and Windus, came in there was something about the off-white matt pages, the typeface, the gravitas of the plain red cover that made me pick it up from the pile of books left in a cardboard box by their previous owner. Tucked inside was a pile of yellowing newspaper articles cut out and folded neatly into the preliminaries of the book. One, possibly taken from a Sunday edition of *The Observer* magazine, focused on the TV production 'Christabel' which starred Elizabeth Hurley (*the* Liz Hurley?) and another two taken from the broadsheet. Carefully pasted underneath the title on the inside page is a black and white photograph of Christabel as a young woman. Why, I wonder, did the owner keep these articles? Were they just simply interested? Did they have English-German fusions in their own family history? Were they even related to the writer? And why is it now that the book has come to us? I put the book aside to take home.

And then, there was the battered paperback copy of Nina Bawden's *The Peppermint Pig*, which looked as if too many primary aged children had handled it. Inside was a slip of paper in a child's handwriting entitled 'They Broke My Heart', which read:

> *I loved her she loved me. I made one mistake and they broke my heart. They sent me to slaughter and that was history for me.*

> *I loved him until he made that one mistake. I didn't care. He broke my ankle and my arm so what I still love him. The next day he wasn't there my dad sent him to slaughter and I never forgave him. He said he was worthless to me.*

Oh dear. That must have been a cheery exercise in reader-response for that kid. Good old teaching technique — i.e. give the child something miserable as it will be good for them and they'll understand that life is not a bed of roses because you only learn through suffering. Wonder if he or she checked out just how life was hanging for those children in their care. Maybe some of them didn't really need a story about a wee pig going to slaughter. I take the slip of paper out of the book. There's no gain for a child to read that.

I don't always take the insertions out of books. I very often leave them in. They belong with the book. They are part of its provenance. Such as the 1936 edition of *A Diary of Private Prayer* which Kelvin weeded out of Religion and was on its way to the recycling boxes when I rescued it. In second-hand book terms it was worthless, Kelvin had priced it at £1 around a year previous and it still had attracted no buyer. But what stayed my hand from skimming it deftly into the recycle boxes was the handwritten piece of paper pasted inside the shabby front board. I was feeling tired after my first full day back at work after a horrible 'flu bug and it now being 4.45pm was looking forward to shutting the shop up soon. Somehow the first line of the extract of poetry — 'Say not the struggle naught availeth' — resonated with my tired being. And how beautiful that language is, how dignified the register. I sat down on the chair by the till and read on. The poem or prayer was apparently by an Arthur Hugh Clough. I reached over to the computer and googled him. Apparently a muscular Christian, published poet and translator, friend of Jane and Thomas Carlyle and secretary to Florence Nightingale. Clough seems to have lived life deeply but it wasn't that that interested me. It was more that this snippet of his writing had been copied out and pasted into what must have been a well used prayer book. A sticker in the top right hand corner of the title page declared that it had been the property of a Church of Scotland minister in Perth. The book was pocket size and I imagined it had indeed spend many years in a coat pocket, faithfully carried and brought out when elevated and comforting words were needed. I liked this. Although we should presume professional religious folk are prayerful, are spiritual, I don't think this is necessarily the case. But here was evidence that at some time there had been a prayerful man quietly going about administering to the vulnerable, adding comfort, perhaps sustaining his own questioning qualms, and that, surely, can only be to the good.

Other inserts into books also take my imagination on journeys. Like an 1895 edition of *The Poetical Works of Walter Scott* which, while cleaning, I found contained in it tiny pressed flowers — a delicate fern and a wee gowan. Did the owner deliberately use this heavy book as a useful tome for pressing flowers? I think not. There are not enough of them and the flowers are not that unusual. I think rather that someone has sat somewhere outside — maybe near Abbotsford — or in countryside figured in one of Scott's many novels — and has paused in their reading, to look up, to gaze, to ponder. Then, when the warmth of the afternoon sun is waning, has reached out, and wi lightsome heart pu'd a wee flooer to mark their page, closed the book and placed it down, still slightly dazed from the doings of Edward Waverley, Fergus and Flora MacIvor, Rose Bradwardine, Evan Dhu Maccombich and Davie Gellatley.

An insert that caught the attention of Kelvin was a letter, dated November 1959 and printed on official hospital paper, a local hospital, which has now closed. He found it in a rather nice copy of *Crowned Masterpieces of Eloquence* by David Josiah Brewer, which, considering the mastery of language displayed in the letter inserted, was a little ironic. Written in large quite painful script, the epistle read:

> *Dear Robert,*
>
> *I hope you received the last letter I had send you, what wrong you haven't been up to see me it about two months and three weeks you haven't seen me, Please try and come up on Saturday and every Saturday, now come up or I be angry. The weather here is bit cold,. I have been out today with two girlfriends.*
>
> *Yours Truly,*
>
> *Susan*

Robbie, my advice to you old chap, is 'stay away'. She ain't in any mood to see and forgive. But who is the 'she'? The writing isn't that of a child but it is that of someone not all that well educated — the confusion of punctuation tells me that even though she did spell 'received' correctly. She has also begun her note with 'I' which in this twenty-first century familiarity with text-speak and social networking is acceptable (although it would probably be lower case if texted by a teenager), but in her day she must have been in receipt of a dominie saying 'Never begin a letter with 'I''. Or was she just so mad that she didn't care for the more formal opening salutations? She certainly isn't a happy lady with this here Robert. Would she have been a patient? Did patients get access to hospital paper? They may have done as printed across the top of the page is the helpful information *'Patients may be visited on any Saturday between 2 and 5pm'*. Only Saturdays are mentioned. What happens on the other days? Or has the epistle perhaps been written by a nurse desperately trying to keep her eyelids from closing during the wee sma hours of night-duty? Is Robert a chap she met at the dancing who swore eternal love to her, then hasn't been seen since? I wonder too if English is not the first language of the nurse or the patient. The 'what wrong' is strong evidence of that. Or maybe the poor lass is in a lot of pain and every drag of the pencil is sore. And why was it is that particular book and why was it kept? Did the book belong to Robert. Did he go and see her? Was it too late? Such mystery. Such mystery.

And then there are the travel books. Occasionally we come across the wonderful Baedekers. When this happens I immediately hear Forster's opinionated and bossy character, Eleanor Lavish, as played by Judi Dench in the Merchant Ivory film version, who refuses to allow the trembling 'cousin Charlotte' use of this safety-blanket for all Victorian travellers, and advises that they will 'simply drift'. Baedekers are always well-thumbed, their pages usually foxed, their information out-dated, but nevertheless still emanating solemnity and reassurance. And they still sell, not so much for their contained information, but for their authenticity. To date I haven't found old cigar-stained railway tickets for the Orient Express, a stubb for the Vienna opera house or a receipt from a reputable mantua-maker, in any, but I live in hope.

By contrast, chunky contemporary guides by the Lonely Planet or Cadogan people can present themselves in pristine condition. Their spines still stiff having hardly been consulted. Did the traveller not actually go then? Or, were they in the company of a native speaker and had no need of the book? Other guides, slight editions useful for carrying in a back pocket, are slightly curled at the edges, some pages circled in pen with exclamation marks and the traces of coffee or wine stains. The books sold to us by a local-born poet, were all like this — particularly the listings for restaurants. Would be a bit of a giggle, and possibly slightly worry him, to ask him how he enjoyed the delights of a particular off-the-beaten track establishment in Andalusia. Some previous owners have thoughtfully left bus timetables inserted, or cards for exhibitions they have enjoyed. I leave some of these in but not all — surely timetables will change? I wonder too why the owners have kept the wee cards for cafes and bars and other attractions. Did they intend to go back there again? Do they think they will be useful for other travellers? Are they a bit of a badge of achievement? I must check my own travel guides at home and see what I have retained. Probably just a few notes saying 'Rubbish! No cludgies!' or some other warnings.

The travel guides I particularly like are the nostalgic ones delineating a time when travel was elegant, planned, unhurried. These books make me think of the 'motoring trip' undertaken by the ageing butler in Ishiguro's tightly controlled comedy of manners, *The Remains of the Day*. Mr Stevens, (do we ever get to know his first name?), superbly played by Anthony Hopkins in the 1993 Merchant Ivory version, says he prefers the undemonstrative environs of the rolling English countryside as against the unrestrained peaks of Scotland or Wales. Well *he* would, wouldn't he? Set in the dying throws of the great houses of England's gentry, the travel scenes in the novel depict an England of hedgerows, cathedrals, country pubs, home-reared sausages and quality mustard. I find the same framing of time in *Bath and Wells*, published by Blackie & Son in 1914, originally priced one shilling. The book forms part of their series 'Beautiful England' and includes serene watercolour illustrations of gently flowing rivers, intricate preserved architecture of palaces and ancient places of worship found in the two old towns. A reader has left a clutch of old pamphlets, price 3d. One is 'Brief Notes concerning the Pump Room, Roman Baths, Banqueting Room'. Another, 'The City of Wells', is apparently the 'Official Guide free on application to the Town Clerk's Office'. Ah, such were the days when you knew what a town clerk was, where to find him and what time he took lunch. This pamphlet is off-set with black and white photographs of the still standing almshouses, inns, market places of the town and the curiosities of the strange rocky gorges, caves, wooded coombs in the easily accessible surroundings. I want to go there. But I want it to look like it does in the pamphlets and book — lovely, dreamy, enduring, quintessential. If only. Today, I know without going there, the old high streets and market places will, must, contain a Starbucks or Costa, surely a MacDonalds and an endemic Tesco. Whip-cracking around the towns will be a ring-road and constant streams of traffic. I wonder what Mr Stevens would have made of his understated England now. I leave the pamphlets in the book — they belong together. They will be safe with each other.

Postcards or notelets are favourite lingerers in books. Some postcards are more memorable than others. Such as the one written from somewhere in Germany from a chap called Peter to a woman called Mrs John Porter (wonder what her own name was?...dear patriarchy, so clever at erasing women). Intelligent sloping handwriting. It said something about how lucky he felt to be travelling in Germany and seeing all he was seeing and experiencing. The line that made my spirit sigh was the last one, which said '*I wish you were happy.*' Oh, why is she not happy? Why is she sad? What has happened? If he had written 'I wish you happiness,' one would presume he was travelling to get over a broken heart that she was marrying this John Porter. But no, he wishes that she was happy. Having ditched him, had she then gone off with someone else, maybe a little more dashing who also owned his own car? Then, later, did she realise the error of her ways? Did she tell Peter, but he, being an honourable gentleman, had replied 'No! it cannot be! You belong to another now!' or some equally frustrating noble declaration, and had refused to take her back? The style of the postcard looks like 1950s. Over sixty years ago. Did she remain unhappy? Did her life get better? Did Peter think 'Stuff the honour code. I'm going to get her?' Did he? Did he? Ah me, I'm never going to know.

I came across another poignant postcard a little while later. This one, which depicted an elevated shot of a very sepia tinged Edinburgh, was addressed to a house named 'Simla' in Shropshire — shades of the Empire there, what? The red one penny stamp carried the bearded head of King George V. Written in very small, neat, mostly legible handwriting, it said:

> *My Dear James, Beans or Spuds.*
>
> *You will be pleased to hear that I today, scaled the heights of Arthur's Seat and obtained a photo from the top. James, old man, I should shout for joy if you walked into my hotel door now. [One presumes he means 'through the hotel door' unless of course he is always up for comic effect.] This is a very beautiful city, with plenty of interesting sights, but, even so, one can feel very lonely, and just at the moment I could do with a 'pal' to share the fun.*
>
> *Hope to see you all again before very long,*
>
> *Kindest regards,*

The signature has been obscured by a corner mount, but it looks like 'Henry'. The card also carries the intriguing postscript:

> *I also presented my compliments at the castle this morning much to their surprise and delight.*

What's all this about? Who is the author that is on familiar terms with whoever was in residence in Holyrood castle? The message is prefigured with the date 25.8.31. Eight years before Britain declared war on Germany and the staging of all that subsequent craziness. The writer is fit and young enough to scale the sharp rise of Arthur's Seat, his writing is controlled and not the shake of an elderly hand. I imagine a tweed clad, straight backed, clipped moustached, stiff-upper-lip chappy in his late thirties or early forties, perhaps home on leave from his posting in the far east. Able. Capable. In control of his life but carrying an unfulfilled heart yearning for 'a pal'. Was 'James', I ponder, just a pal? If life were different for both of them, would he be more? And why was this postcard kept? And why has it landed in our shop? Questions. Questions.

And then there are the inserts into books which jolt your memory right back to childhood. On picking up a fairly battered edition of Dean's *Superb Book for Girls*, the following scene elicited:

'*Scraaaaps! Scraaaaaps!*'

'What?' says Kelvin. 'What?'

'Scraps! You know...*Scraaaaps!*' I elucidate.

'And they're interesting because...?' enquires Kelvin.

'Because they're *Scraaaaps!*' I counter.

'Right. I'll wait till you calm down then I'll ask you again,' says Kelvin and walks off.

I sit down on the nearest chair and flip through the book which I note was published in 1964. I would have been two years old. Too young to be collecting scraps. That didn't happen till I was probably at least six or seven.

'Is there an Angel?' I wonder unconsciously holding my breath as I turn the rough pages.

What are these? A wee collection of Cinderellas at the ball, carefully preserved in a clear cellophane bag. *Mmmm*, don't remember them. Pinocchio and Jimmy Cricket — they were never my favourites. A wee cutsie girl with a flower pot helmet, didn't collect her either. Boys in knickerbocker trousers with lace collars (really?) carrying a rose plant and a card —dull, dull. Some cut out pictures of a performing seal — they're not real scraps! A Noddy, I remember him. Another Big and a Wee Boy with ankle socks, polished shoes, slicked back hair carrying huge bunches of Marguerites — they look really poncy now. And yes! Yes! An Angel! Not the Big One, just a Medium size and The Tottie One. Someone has written 'NO!' on the back of the medium size angel. Oh, yes, we did that didn't we? You wrote 'NO!' so the person avidly flicking through your book would know that one wasn't up for swaps. What else is there? Ah, a Medium and a Wee Amy Johnson in her aircraft flying (amazingly) with garlands of roses around her, her goggles up on her hat despite the fact that the blades are whirring. What were the designers thinking of? ... What else?... A Big and a Wee Santa! This lass has worked hard. They were almost *never* up for swaps. Ah, but yes, she's written 'NO' on the big one. Sensible. And...some Clowns doing gymnastics — was never into them. And ... another Angel!!! I can't read what has been written on the back. Looks like '*Hosanna*' — did the Angels have different names then? But the Wee One says '*Don't send back*'. She must have lent her book to a pal. You only did that with best pals, you couldn't trust anyone else. Oh, more of those chubby Wee Boys with ankle socks and flowers, they're still in the original packet. Either she liked these or couldn't get rid of them. And ... joy of joys! The Medium Basket of Flowers with 'NO' on the back. I liked them. They were good. More Clowns and singing frogs. Singing frogs? Don't remember them. The story of Red Riding Hood in press-outs. Didn't do her either. Another lovely Angel dressed in a lovely blue gown and carrying lilies ——very Virgin Mary. I bet I liked that one. Now this is weird … three looking-glass portraits of a very young Queen Elizabeth (II of England, I of Scotland — let's get it right), a toddler Princess Anne and a round-cheeked Prince Charles. I never had them. Don't think I would have wanted them. They are too real. Scraps belong to fantasy. Now here's a doll-like Girl carrying a staring eyed Sailor doll with the words '*Might*' scribbled out and '*NO!*' put in. More kids and flowers and … *ooooh* … the figures in national dress from various countries. The Scottish Dancer has '*NO!*' on its back — quite right — the Hawaiian Dancer with her grass skirt and neck garland and not a lot else, hasn't anything written. Bet I was never allowed to have that one. This lass is obviously hopeful of swapping her too. The Japanese, Irish, Italian all say '*NO!*' and the Russian has '*NO, NO, NO, NO, NO!*' — ah, the pick of the crop. Can't remember how much she must have been worth? Four other scraps maybe? What else? About a dozen Flower Baskets with one that says '*It doesn't matter*' — yes, that's a boring one. Some cut-outs from what must have been a Brownie Guide mag — they're not proper scraps either. They were just to bulk out your collection. A Robin Hood and some of the Merry Men and Sheriff of Nottingham. No '*NO!*' on the back of these, too boyish for girls who did Scraps. A few faces of Angels. I quite liked those. They were cheery and good currency too.

I've reached the end of the book. I look up. See that I am still in the bookshop. I was far ben there. Way way back to the street where I grew up with my best pal, Joan McKee, across the road and another pal, Kim Gibson, who got new Scraps all the time because she was an-only-child-and-spoilt. And the big dictionary that I used to keep my Scraps in till it got too heavy to cart around and I changed to something else. And Langies or 'Langmuir Stores' as we were told to call it, who sold the Scraps. You fished them out of a wonderful rummage box that had *everything* in it. But mostly we just swapped. Sometimes I took a few

of mine to school and swapped. I don't think I took my big dictionary
— that was just for home and the street. That was for keeping your
precious collection in and for pouring over while you murmured, 'Yes.
Swap. Swap. Swap. No. Don't Swap. Don't Swap. Swap. Swap. Swap.
Wish I had ...'

The shop door jingles. Cassie comes in.

'Phew,' she says 'I've been everywhere today.'

I don't answer but just point to the book on the table in front of me.

'Have a look at this,' I say. 'I'll get your coffee.'

'What is it?' she says 'An old children's book? Looks like there's
something in it ... Oooooooh, Scraaaaaps!'

Kelvin groans. 'What is it with you wummin and scraps?' he says.

'They're Scraaaaps!' we both answer.

'Has it got the Big Angel?' asks Cassie.

Kelvin groans again. There are some things men just don't get.

Things left in books can also be quite profitable. Such as the time I
noticed a book on tracing one's family history left lying on the table. I
was busy at the time searching for a copy of Orwell's *Animal Farm* for
a secondary pupil. As I passed the table I thought I glimpsed money
sticking out of the top edge of the book. The shop was fairly busy and,
thinking that perhaps one of the customers nearest the table had left
their money there with the intention of buying the book, I carried on
doing what I was doing. A mobile phone rang and a customer answered
it, exclaimed and swiftly made his way out of the shop. Other customers
moved around, bought or didn't buy books, and left the shop. I passed

the table again. The book was still there. I boxed up some books for recycling and came back into the main area to find Cassie had arrived. She poured herself some coffee and moved towards the table.

'Is that ... Is that *money* in that book?' she asked.

'Yeh, I was wondering that,' I said and called out 'Anyone left a book on family history on the table?'

No answer. The shop is empty apart from me and Cassie.

Cassie opened the book. Three £20 notes are sitting there.

'Ooooh, £60!' she says. 'Right, I'm a witness that we've found it. What'll you do with it?'

I have a fleeting desire to say 'Hey, let's you and I go out for a slap-up lunch,' but of course don't. Ah me. Why was I brung up so ethical? So instead I say 'Um, let's take the cash out, put it in the counter drawer and see what happens.'

'Look,' says Cassie, passing me the money 'look at the page the money was marking. It says 'Researching family history will cost you money.' Ha ha! Damn right! £60 for whoever left it there.'

We giggle and go on to blether about other matters. Cassie has her coffee, munches her favourite 'Pengi' biscuit — having already donated a full pack to the coffee cupboard — and then trots off.

Ten minutes later the door opens and a man comes in and makes his way directly to the table. He spies the book, lifts it, shakes it then looks at me.

'Did you leave money in that?' I ask, careful not to specify how much.

'No. I found some in it. I was going to tell you but my phone rang and there was an emergency at work. I was halfway there when I remembered

I hadn't told you about the money.'

'That's very decent of you,' I say 'You could have gone out for a wee shopping spree with what was in there.'

'Aye. £60 wasn't it? I was just shaking it to see if there was anymore.'

I make a mental note to always shake books.

'But I want to buy the book anyway. It looks interesting.'

'Sir,' I say 'I think the book's yours. A wee reward for your honesty.'

'Not at all. How much is it? £2.50? Here you are.'

'Nope. I'm not taking it. That's yours. I would give you the money you found but the owner of it may still turn up.'

'And I wouldn't take the money if you did. It's not mine. I wisnae brought up tae take what isnae mine,' he says in an obvious echo of a douce Scots grannie waggling her boney finger at him.

Who says honourable gentlemanly form is dead?

'Quite right,' I reply. 'And it will come back to you of course,' I say. 'The effect of your good deed I mean … that's how it works …'

'Mmmm,' he says 'never thought of it like that. Mmmm.'

He grins, tucks the book under his arm and leaves the shop. I wonder what further return he will get for his honesty.

Meantime, £60. That's my day's wage and some of tomorrow's covered. Thank you previous owner. I hope your family history merited the loss. Or were you making a gesture of atonement for their sins?

Inscriptions

Now these often prove to be real curios. Not necessarily the work of lapidary but nonetheless they do engrave an important snippet of the owner's story. I love the formal ones found in books given as school prizes. Weren't they were the days! Now I suppose it would be an iTunes token or some other C21 appropriate mark of approval. Here's an example of what used to happen … In an old Collins edition of *Tom Brown's School Days* there is a slip pasted onto the front endpaper which announces it was presented to '*Maggie Quinn, Qualifying Class C*, by '*The Eastwood School Board of Shawlands Academy*' as a prize '*for Regular Attendance*'. Did that make her heart sing I wonder? Did the very fact that she had got a prize make her smile? Did she have any other books at home? 'Regular Attendance' is, well, creditable I suppose, unless you are being telt to go to the school even if your ear-ache is drilling your head in half or your temperature is way beyond normal. Wonder if Maggie thought all those freezing winter mornings chipping ice off the top of your bottle of free milk was worth this prize? I rather think a few more mornings tucked up cosy in bed might have been preferred.

Then there are the inscriptions on books given as gifts. On a rather scruffy hardback edition of *Highlands of Scotland* by Hugh Quigley published by Scribner's in 1936, is the flowing hand, fountain-penned inscription: '*To Aunt Evelyne, with love Cedric*'. I would hazard a guess that Cedric gave this to his aunt because of her love of holidaying in Scotland. How do I deduce this? Elementary. We are short on Cedrics in Scotland, whereas they are more plentiful south of the border. And a lad who has an aunt who has the leisure to read about Auld Scotia also suggests she was an educated woman. An educated woman who maybe kept a wee hoose amang the heather as an annual bolt-hole, maybe for when the grouse were in season. Perhaps I haver. Perhaps I don't. It's still rather touching though that a young blister of a nephew has thought enough of his old auntie to go out, select, buy and send her a present for her birthday. Did she perhaps knit socks and Fair-Isle sleeveless jumpers for his birthday? I'll be able to deduce this if I find another inscription from our Ced on a book of vintage knitting patterns.

Another inscription has been composed on very faint pencil lines drawn so to keep one's handwriting neat, presentable. The writing is stiff and constrained — the writing of someone taught to write with the constant threat of a sharp belt of a ruler across one's knuckles if you made a mess and strayed outside the proscribed lines. My father's writing was like this. Although in some ways it was quite perfect — the tail ends of each letter perfectly formed and every word perfectly legible — to the end of his days he found writing difficult, cumbersome, taxing. The precision of forming the words deterred him from the unconscious flow of the pen keeping pace with his thoughts. Instead any missive was carefully thought about, reviewed in his head, thought about again, then finally written down. He watched me once while I was scribbling something down — and it was a scribble — and said 'I envy you your writing. You seem to find it so easy'. The ironic thing now is that my handwriting, unless I concentrate very hard, is almost illegible — too many years of frantically trying to capture the salient points of lectures, seminars, workshops, speeches. My further excuse is that with the advent of the computer and mobile phone, with their accoutrements of email and texting, it is rare than I actually have to write anything more than a shopping list. So now, when I have to write something that must be clear to the reader — a greetings card, a postcard, a note to our dog walker, an inscription to someone in a book — my hand stiffens, especially when I am tired and my muscle memory is poor, and, if not careful to consciously relax my hand, write a little bigger, form the letters into understandable shapes while retaining my own individual preference for a slope to the right, it can come out like the script issued from a demented and hallucinatory mind. As Kelvin remarked recently in his usual diplomatic manner, while trying to make sense of an entry penned by me in the shop diary, 'What is this meant to say? Looks like you've been chiselling instead of writing'.

The inscription then on the title page of Archie Cameron's *Bare Feet and Tackety Boots* published by Luath Press in 1988, with its carefully drawn pencil lines, is perhaps then not such a bad idea. Maybe I should adopt this praxis until I relearn how to write. This book is signed by the author — at least it appears to be so, it is really impossible to verify this unless great and detail research is done — and in slightly shaky script says, '*To a dear friend of long standing who's insouciant attitude to the vicissitudes of life is remarkable.*' Now, isn't that elegantly put? Wouldn't you like to be told that your nonchalance, your ease, your sanguine attitude to the ups and downs of life has been noted and deemed worthy? And those lovely, almost archaic words, 'insouciant', 'vicissitudes', that roll around the tongue and teeth and speak of classical thought, culture and Stephen Fry, are just wonderful. I must take note. I have tended towards the rather more prosaic 'Hope you enjoy. Best Wishes, Anne'. Perhaps I should work on some carefully thought out wording which would suggest that I have put more than a modicum of effort into it.

Kelvin hands me a three volume set of Walter Scott's *Tales of a Grandfather*.

'These are quite nice. See if you can find a place on the shelf for them,' he says.

I glance over at the Scott shelf, it is pretty jammed but perhaps with a careful bit of manoeuvring, it may be possible. I have a look at the books, checking if they need cleaned. Kelvin has already priced them at £15 for the three volumes. Seems fine to me. The books, published by Gowans and Grey in 1923 are blue boarded, their edges tanned, pages rough cut, their insides are clean with a small amount of foxing, their binding is still fairly tight. I flip to the preliminaries of each volume and see someone has penned an inscription in flowing fountain pen on each title page. Volume 1 says 'Many Happy Returns from Helen'; Volume 2 says 'A Book, a Fire, a Dream – These Three' and Volume 3 says 'Many Happy Hours'. All three inscriptions are dated 28th January 1939. Nine months before the outbreak of the Second World War. Did Helen know it was coming? Was this perhaps the last gift she may have given a beloved one? Was her dream that it all would never happen? Did she and the birthday person survive it all and remain unscathed just as these books have done. I wonder. If books could but talk.

I flick the pastry brush along their spines, removing any lingering dust, squirt some gentle cleaning liquid onto a cloth and carefully wipe the boards, then, moving other books out of the way, place them together on the shelf where they can wait quietly for a new owner who may recognise the lasting value of 'a book, a fire, a dream'.

Carriers and Couriers

Books arrive in the shop in a variety of ways, or rather by a variety of means. We have learned to connect the mode of carrier with the quality of books. For example, black plastic big bags heaved through the doorway by a disgruntled person are invariably bad news. Black bins bags means the owner or courier cares not a jot about books and has shoved them in any old how, leaving the spines to crack, edges to curl and often, very often, has even left them in some damp garage or cellar or car boot to moulder until they find time to bring them to us. Sometimes they smell of cigarette smoke, sometimes they are grotty dirty. Why the heaver thinks that we will want them is beyond my comprehension. The only answer I can come up with is that they think we love all books with an egalitarian passion and any offerings are welcome. How deluded can you get? Nine times out of ten, when the person has deposited their load, been told the books are worthless or given some silly sum of money, we rapidly sift through them, fling the majority straight into our recycling boxes and then scrub down our hands. Not the most pleasant aspect of working in a bookshop.

A more promising plastic bag is that of the durable type sold for 20p or so in supermarkets. Being stronger they offer more protection to books and it says to us that the seller has done something towards presenting the books nicely. They usually want the bags back too — which can be viewed as admirable in that they are therefore saying that they will use them again, or simply that, having paid the vast sum of 20p, they are going to get their money's worth.

Another favourite mode of transport is the small battered backpack: out of which can come a surprising amount of volumes such as Manga comics and graphic novels. This seller is very often an avid collector of some series or other and what they are selling to us are those they judge of little or no value. Sometimes though, it is genuinely that they need the money. Like the young student who told me he was short by 10p of his bus to university, who looked as if a good three course breakfast wouldn't go amiss, and who was having to live on his wits until money from his mum would arrive. Maybe it was a story, but as I am also the mum of a young man trying to cut it in today's world, I admired the student's ingenuity and along with the couple of quid for his books I also gave him a banana and told him to eat it before he did anything else. I swear he almost answered 'Thanks mum' before he grinned and headed off hopefully in time for his lecture.

The bags carried by older people — you know those proper 'shopper' type made of hessian or leather — usually emit a half dozen or so Catherine Cookson, Lee Child, Mills and Boon, or James Patterson. The desired deal here is that the person wants to do a swap — offering their read titles for a title they are seeking. This barter kind of transaction takes a little bit of careful handling as a newer customer will sometimes expect that they can use the shop like a library and six books *in* qualifies them for six books *out*. I used to waste a lot of breath explaining that the shop can't run on these lines, that the owner has to pay rent, rates, bills and staff wages etc. This usually resulted with blank incomprehension and the question 'So how many *can* I have then?' Now I just say assertively, after glancing at the condition of the proffered books, 'That's fine. You can take a free book in return,' and carry on with whatever I had been doing. For the first time 'lender' who is slightly pit oot that their books are not better currency, I smile and say 'there's a library just up the road'.

Cardboard boxes. Strangely enough we don't get that many of these. People will often describe their books as being 'one or two boxes' on the phone but when they come this manifests as either small plastic crates (which they always want back) or strong bags. Occasionally they lurch in with the open bread-basket type of box. These open crate-like boxes contain items collected from car boot sales, the spines are displayed upwards so we can see the titles which the seller hopes are tempting. The books are clean. There are pamphlets too — sights of old Aberdeen, Forfar, Arbroath etc / football programmes / guide books to Scottish castles / art exhibitions. You get to know the regular sellers and those whose books don't need checking as they will be both interesting and clean. This type of seller knows the shop, knows our prices, knows what to tempt us with, already has a ball-park sum of money in their mind which they are happy to accept and which we will try to weedle out if we can be bothered. Half the time I suspect this type of seller is really there for the fun of the thing and if they can make a few bob then that's all to the good.

A little more rare and also more unwelcome, are old suitcases. These almost always contain dusty and damp books from 'Uncle Jimmy's / Aunt Mary's loft' which 'have been there for years and probably worth a lot of money...', or so the seller expects. There's always a bible, some old travel books, Walter Scott novels, maybe a Mrs Beeton and other curiosities — invariably water-stained with curled boards, all dusty, mostly mouldy. Had they been in better condition they could well be valuable, but in most cases (no pun intended), the state of the books means they do a hop, skip and jump into our recycle boxes. If Kelvin is not in, I have become quite deft at skimming the books frisbee-fashion straight into the waiting boxes. The seller often wants to gift us the suitcases too. What we are supposed to do with them is not quite clear. In the early days I used to try to help people out — I felt sorry for those clearing out the house of a gone-to-glory relative or family friend. Now, having heard these tales a hundred times or more, I just smile sympathetically but hand the suitcases back with a firm 'There's a charity shop just down the road which might be grateful for them'. Bet they're not, but that's their problem.

Other books are more ingenious and spurn traditional modes of arrival. Such as the time I heard a faint shout outside the door, dismissed it as that of a restless native, and carried on wedging more poetry into the shelves. The shout went up again and a customer popped his head into the Poetry aisle saying 'There's a wummin out here that needs help…'. I left Wordsworth where he was and skipped to the door wondering what scenario would greet me. Outside is an elderly woman bundled up in a motorised wheelchair who is smiling and holding out a plastic bag.

'Here you are hen, they'll maybe be of some good to you. Ah've finished with them.'

'Are you just handing them in?'

'Aye. Didn't want to gie them to a charity shop. Thought youse would like them.'

'That's really kind. Thank you for making the effort.'

'Nae bother hen. Nae bother. Cheerio.'

She puts her chair into First and zooms away, bouncing over the uneven pavement scattering all dawdlers like Moses parting the Red sea.

I look in the bag. Six Martina Cole books and not in great condition. I think of the herculean effort to get them to us and decide I will do my best to salvage at least a couple.

Perhaps the most unusual mode of travel was that of dog baskets.

'Don't laugh,' said the woman as she staggered through the door. 'It's all I could find and I did hoover them out before I put the books in.'

'That's more than some folks would do,' I reply.

The books aren't too bad. Mostly 'family' books, the type someone gets you at Christmas when they haven't a clue what to buy — guides to the best way to do yoga, bird-watching, DIY, card games, needlepoint and flower arranging, also a couple of new looking *Poems on the Underground* as well as two dog-training books.

'Did it work?' I ask, pointing to the dog books.

'Not really,' she sighs.

Now dogs are a subject I don't mind pausing for. Specially if the other half of the conversation strikes me as vaguely intelligent. My husband is a Dog Listener trained in the Amichien philosophy of Jan Fennell and spends much of his time sorting out ingrained myths that humans hold about dogs. But in the fact that the woman is using two dog baskets, two *empty* dog baskets, I check my impulse to rush in with my usual thesis on dog behaviour and promotion of Colum's business and ask:

'And do you still have the dogs?'

'Oh yes, they're still with us, totally mental both of them, but I got them some lovely comfy basket-weave beds to encourage them to relax and so don't need these. Do you want them?'

My mind flickers to what Kelvin might say if he discovers two big plastic dog beds in the back store. Could be worth a wind-up. I could tell him that I have decided to bring my two Collies in as a security measure on days when I am working on my own. Oh, that would be such fun.

The woman sees my hesitation, misconstrues it as possibility and ploughs on.

'They're still very good, seems a shame to ditch them.'

I give up on the idea of winding up Kelvin and look at the beds. They are actually in not too bad a nick. We don't need them at home but I wonder about my husband's clients. Maybe someone would be grateful for them. Colum would probably be in the shop at lunchtime and could get them in the car before Kelvin clocks them. So, against my usual hardline policy, I hear myself say:

'Ok, leave them here and I'll see if I can redistribute them.'

She goes off happy to be free of books and dog baskets. In exchange I did manage to off-load a couple of Colum's business cards. I somehow don't think the introduction of nice crisp basket-weave beds will do much to help the dogs' stress levels. My experience is that dogs find them a rather useful gnawing board when worried. But heh, that's not my problem at the moment.

An hour later I see Colum chaining up his bike outside and pulling out of a pannier what looks like cartons of soup. He comes into the shop and I greet him with:

'Hi. Look at these. Good as new really. Want them for a client?'

He flicks his eyes over the baskets.

'No thanks,' he says.

'No? Really? There's not much wrong with them,' I persist.

'Maybe, but I don't need them,' he says and goes down the corridor to put the kettle on.

Hell's teeth. I now need to get rid of two large dog baskets before Kelvin comes in later. I consider running to the charity shop with them while Colum is in the shop but, at that precise moment, the door jangles and a Frequent Flyer appears who wants me to search for a book on the internet for him. This takes a while and when he finally leaves there is now no time for me to run anywhere. I decide that I'll just have to put up with Kelvin's lecture on not allowing customers to leave luggage in the shop and, when he runs out of steam, tell him I will stick them in our car and deposit them in the nearest charity shop when I can.

This decided I sit down to drink my lukewarm soup. Just as I am swilling down the last mouthful, a woman appears enquiring about some local history books. We blether about our town, the demise of the mills and the lack of a definitive user-friendly-not-too-expensive-explanatory-volume on the poetry of Tannahill. She browses about a bit and then selects two books. Coming up to the counter she then notices the dog baskets which are still sitting with their cargo of books.

'Are they dog baskets?' she giggles.

'Sure are,' I say. 'Want them?'

'Do I want them? Are you selling them?'

'Not selling, giving, it's a bit of a story, but they're free to a good home.'

'Really. Now, that's amazing because I actually do need a dog basket.'

'Just one? You can have both.'

'No, I only need one.'

I look at the books on the counter.

'Tell you what, if you take both the baskets you can have one of these books free.

Yes, I'm wheedling and being decidedly pushy. But I really could do without the Kelvin lecture.

'Done,' she says.

Yeh!

I ring up the price of one book, put it in a clean plastic bag. Rapidly empty the dog baskets. Speed is essential, I don't want to create any margin for a change of mind. Stack the baskets one inside the other, pop her book on top and hand her unexpected purchases. She takes the load from me. I go ahead and open the shop door for her.

'I'm presuming you have a car with you,' I say

'Oh yes,' she says 'my husband is parked just over there.' She suddenly giggles, 'He's looking rather puzzled. He's checking the name of the shop. I told him I just wanted to pickup something on local folklore…'

'Just tell him we are a rather unusual bookshop,' I say.

'Yes, you certainly are,' she says, 'it'll make a good story.'

'Ah, yes,' I agree.

The Internet Doesn't Smell As Good

I doubt a week goes by in Cloisters without someone raising the subject. On the first few occasions I found it interesting, thought-provoking, as I mentally masticated the chewy points while enjoying the company of a like-minded reader. But after, say, the first ten such conversations which often ended up as point-scoring against the insidious and invisible enemy, I unconsciously shortened the allotment of time I was willing to donate to the discourse. Not that it's not a relevant subject. Quite the reverse. It is a most relevant subject considering it takes place in a bookshop. Nowhere could be more relevant. It's just that I started to get a bit bored with rehearsing the arguments again and again and again. It began to feel exhaustive. Each customer clearly wanted to air their view with people in the actual business and had perhaps saved up their choice statements to share with us, confident that we would solidly concur. I began to wonder though if it would be better to print out a big poster with our mission statement on it — to which we could point — and the customer could then say something like 'Yip, I'm on the same page,' and he or she would be free to get on with browsing the books and we could get on with what we do with them. What am I talking about? The e-book discussion of course, or 'the EBD' as I now think of it.

Last week for example, a chap who had been in the shop for fifteen minutes or so, strolled past the counter where I was listing some books for Amazon sales, and said, apparently to no-one in particular:

'No, just don't get it.'

'Sorry, did you say something?'

'I said I just don't get it. No. No. Particularly when in a place like this.'

Ah, I recognise the opening moves here and wait for more. More there will be. Assistance is not required.

'I mean, you come in here and you're surrounded by the real thing. The real thing. You can pick them up, they have shape, texture, colour and they are all different. You don't get that with the e-book.'

'No, you don't.'

I could say more. Of course I could say lots and lots more but I have a job to do and, given a soupçon of encouragement, this topic will run. I do smile though — but the smile works in the same way as a full stop does in a sentence. It's delineating the end of something.

'And, I don't know about you, but I notice that I can't remember all the books I've read if I read them in electronic format.'

Now, actually this is a point I haven't heard before. Yes … *mmmm* … it's true. I think about how I remember books. I see their shape, their front cover — albeit hazy sometimes. I see the size, the depth. I remember any artistic endpapers or gum and ink marbled boards. I remember the colours of the edges — faded gold for old classics, occasionally red or black or purple for cute hardback editions of poetry or prose, re-issues by a publisher hoping to rekindle interest (*oooh* … an unintentional double entendre?) In particular I see the spines, that part of a book being most often on display. I see the trademark forest green of Virago Modern Classics; the cool dove grey of a Persephone edition; the differing but distinctive Penguin mass market paperbacks; the gravitas of a late nineteenth century Macmillan or Blackwood gilt-tooled volume; the cloth-boarded Folio titles snug in their protective slipcases; the serious informative spines of Canongate Classics; the authoritative black and white blocked spines of Everyman's Library and a whole other myriad of impressions and images. And I see where they are, or should be, on my bookshelves at home or in the shop. Yes, he's earned a comment.

'You're right,' I say. 'The mind needs difference to help it remember. We're complex creatures.'

He rocks back on his heels considering my comment. I worry I have opened the floodgates so smile again and look back at the computer screen.

'Aye, it's all just walls of type. There are some illustrations now, I'll give them that, but nawh, it's all just pretty boring really. I mean look at this. Ye cannae get that wi yer e-version.'

He pulls out one of the books advertised on the shop website — Robert Bell's edited *Golden Leaves from the Works of the Poets and Painters* published by Charles Griffin & Company, c. 1870, in full red leather with gilt edging and rules either side of the raised bands on the spine.

'Now, that's just sheer class. Sheer class. If I had that book I would know I had that book. Just the feel of it is good. Ye cannae feel anything wi the e-book. And ah tell ye whit … the internet just disnae smell as good.'

He's quite right of course. I can't count the number of people who come in the shop for the first time, pause, sniff the air and go '*Aaaaaaah,* old books'.

That's deserving of another comment.

'Yes, we're sensate beings. There's more to the reading experience than gliding your eye and finger over a smooth surface. Depends though why you're reading I guess.'

We ponder this together.

'Aye,' says the chap 'If I jist want information, like on the screen you're looking at, then aye, I can see the point. But if I want to savour something, get lost in it, you need a book book for that.'

I think back to a recent conversation I had had with my brother-in-law. Liam clocked up many years as an academic librarian and, not being a Luddite, is always prepared to give advances in technology a chance. He is currently helping another friend design an e-book lending service for developing countries. A plus I must say for the e-book argument. We had got into a e-book versus real-book discussion and Liam had commented that the way designers and marketers of the e-book needed to go, was to bring the e-book closer to the real book. Look at what people got out of reading a real book, what they liked about it, and simulate that experience if possible. We wondered if, sometime in the future, there would be smell capsules available which would come under the heading 'musty' or 'fag-end' or 'brand new' that you could release on your fingers or into a small bowl to place beside your reading technology, which would enhance the reading experience.

'And what about all the things left in books?' I had said. 'Where will these go? All those bus and train tickets, all those gift cards, shopping lists, photos, postcards, theatre tickets, letters ... all of that. Where will all of that go? And the inscriptions and dedications and bookmarks and bookplates? Everything that tells the provenance of the book, the people it has meant something to, the lives it has touched — none of that has a place in the e-book.'

I don't repeat this though to the chap in front of the counter. He's got his own thoughts, he doesn't need mine too and if I did try to outline them we would be here till next Tuesday. What would he make for example, at the knowledge that my last published book is now being prepared as an e-book? Would he think I had sold out to the enemy?

Would I defend myself and say, that one has to embrace technology and go with publishing practices if not to be left behind? Would I tell him that the e-book version will mean my elderly aunt, who has very little sight left, will be able to enlarge the print size on her e-book reader and so read my book? Would I tell him that this way many more people will read it as the e-version is much cheaper than the paper? Would I tell him that I can capitalise on the impulse-buy facet of the human psyche which wants something now, this moment, and not in a few days' time when the post is delivered? Or would he reason 'Aye well, you can do both — work in a second-hand bookshop, revel in real books, keep a massive pile of them at home, but see the usefulness of the technology of the modern world such as when you have run out of time to buy or borrow your bookgroup book and decide to download it'?

What he would or wouldn't think isn't given a chance to air though as the phone suddenly rings. The person on the end of the line wants to know if we have Eugene O'Neill's play *Long Day's Journey Into Night* in stock and I have to skim up to Drama and do a quick search. While there, two more customers come in and queue up at the counter. Seeing the likelihood of the continuance of our discussion fast diminishing, the 'real book chap', nods at me and makes his way out of the shop. I am quite sure he will be back to continue the philippic another day.

When the shop goes quiet I find myself thinking more about what has happened in the book business and why some of us are struggling with it. As the think tank, the Institute for the Future of the Book, tell us (google them…the irony is not lost on me), books in their print-on-paper format have been with us for the past five hundred years, so it's little wonder that we are oscillating about the worth of the digital future. The main problem for us is that it's all happened so quickly. The galloping growth of the internet in the mid 90s effectively sent what had been a slowly turning publishing business into hyper-speed and the launch of the Sony ebook reader in 2006, and Amazon's Kindle in

2007, marked a watershed in publishing history. Us humans, us bookish humans, are a little thrown by it all. What's that Arabic saying about our soul which travels at the speed of a camel? And books surely have something to say to our souls. Therein lies the rub. Many of us actually care about the future of the book and the correlating reading experience.

There is the environmental argument of course and, if we are concerned about our role as stewards of the earth for the next generation, then we do need to think about this. Trees don't get chopped down to make e-books — although what damaging footprint the production of computers has, needs to be taken into account. And another plus is that one can take the e-book wherever you go — provided the battery lasts, it doesn't inexplicably freeze up and you don't drop it. I think about the time I took the collected letters of Virginia Woolf on holiday to Spain in a silly fit of being an always-on-the-job academic, and it spent the week in my suitcase huge, bulky, unopened while I kept nicking the light paperback of Tony Hawks' *A Piano in the Pyrenees* from my husband whenever he left it down. Had I had access to e-books then I would have been a happier holidaymaker. And I think of the customer who told me that when his train from London to Glasgow came to a sudden and dark halt, which lasted four hours, he had simply turned on his iPad and read one of the books he had already downloaded. The lack of electric light on the train meaning nothing as his technology had its own. The poor traditional readers had sighed, put their books down and stared gloomily at their own reflection in the grimy rain-splattered windows.

I ponder too on the tradition of the book signing. Fairly recently I went along to hear Lesley Riddoch read from and speak about her extended polemic *Blossom: What Scotland Needs to Flourish* (Luath Press, 2013). At the end of what had been a very informative and entertaining event, my husband queued up to buy her book and returned triumphantly with a copy freshly inscribed 'To Anne and Colum, Happy Reading! Yours aye, Lesley Riddoch'. I liked the 'Yours aye' — it suited the subject matter, and immediately made the reader / author relationship into a closer more fond one, despite the fact Ms Riddoch didn't know us from Adam and Eve. Two friends had also come along with us, one of whom had already downloaded an e-version of *Blossom*. 'Are you going to ask her to sign your Kindle?' joked her husband.

There's something too in all of this tussle which concerns identity. As John B Thompson notes in his erudite *Merchants of Culture* (2010), which discusses the publishing business in the twenty-first century, books on display in a home are obviously something valued by the owner and reflect what they deem to matter. They can act therefore as an extension to the mindset of the inhabitants. I deliberately say 'can' here as we certainly have books on our shelves at home that definitely don't reflect my interests — the autobiography *Parky* for example or McGregor and Boorman's blokeish *Long Way Down* and the assortment of John le Carré novels would definitely find themselves in the next charity shop bag if I was allowed. In fairness though I reckon my collections of the writing of Elizabeth von Arnim, Barbara Pym and Carol Shields, the yardage of my 'teaching' books and, most definitely, my knitting pattern books, will also meet the same fate should I shuffle off this mortal coil before my husband. For the moment though the hundredweight of books we currently have in our home reflects who we are as a collective unit. Whereas the blank and silent screen of an inactive e-book tells you precisely nothing. Maybe that's useful. I wonder how many people quietly downloaded *Fifty Shades of Grey* in deliberate preference to buying the paper copy and not therefore having to declare their curiosity? It all becomes a bit more secretive then doesn't it? A bit more private. And all those potential conversations, all those potential meetings between strangers who note the book the other is holding and comment on it, chat about it and (in the film version) go on to fall in love, I presume they happen a lot less these days. What also disappears with the e-book is such sights as seeing four people, seated separately, on the 5.37pm commuter train from

Glasgow to Paisley, all deeply immersed in Dan Brown's *Da Vinci Code* completely unconscious that another three people were also entranced by Langdon and Neveu's frantic investigations and completely oblivious I was observing them. Had I been either the publisher or author of that book I would have been fair chuffed.

My book books also help me think. When I find myself wondering what words to cite in a piece of writing, what book to advise a Higher English student to read, what book to leave beside the bed of a house guest, what book to accompany me on a train or bus journey, what book to climb the golden stairs with, soothe me in the middle of the night or take to a shady nook in the garden, I walk up and down in front of my bookshelves at home. Titles and names jump out at me and I hear words chattering behind their covers. 'Ah yes,' I say 'you'll do.' And I pull out an item which I invariably, in good bookshop training, give a quick dust, before tucking it in my bag, placing it on my desk, or putting it on the lower step of the staircase to the bedrooms. Having only actually read one complete book in electronic version, (honest), I have no accumulated digital library to draw on. And even if I did, I somehow think I wouldn't access it in the same manner. It's not that I am computer adverse. I use a computer to write, to email, to browse the net, to see what my son is up to on Facebook, to do presentations, to send photos, to search and collate information, to play music and the radio, and I find You Tube a great help when struggling to learn the rhythm of a new-to-me piano tune. In my former academic existence I read digital images of Victorian literary magazines on my computer screen which were of tremendous help for a desperate doctoral student. But books, real books, were and still are my preferred choice of medium. There's just something about the thing itself, the artefact. All that craft and skill in one volume.

Which leads me to think of all the skilled people who provide the infrastructure of the book — the talented artists and photographers who help sell a book. The sales of my last book owe much to the eye-catching photographs on the covers gifted to me by my creative son and tastefully displayed by the publisher. A book therefore isn't totally the work of the author, other talents are required to complement and illustrate our words. We work well as a team. And, really, is there really anything as lovely as a beautifully bound and presented book? I dare you not to want to hold it in your hands and turn it over and over. Designers know this — sure they do — why else would the clever bods at Apple sell covers for laptops, iPads, and iPhones that imitate old dyed morocco or calf-skin books which people buy to add a touch of class to their gizmo? A thing of beauty, ladies and gentlemen, will always be a thing of beauty.

And is there a child in the world who doesn't want to run their hand over the picture while the words are being read to them? How would teachers of young children cope without those outsize picture books they hold up for all to see? Passing round the Kindle is just unworkable. Some books for pre-school kids are designed to be touched — material of different types is incorporated into the book. And what of the brilliant pop-up book? Can the e-book do that?

Perhaps though it's the old adage of horses for courses. My husband and I are not great fans of home decorating. We have to sit ourselves down, sigh a lot, plan a weekend we are both free, ring-fence it in the diary, swear hand-on-heart not to accept any other more tempting invites and go and buy some paint. Then I schedule in a trip to our local library where I pick up at least three audio books. The audio books raise what could be a tedious chore to that of a fairly pleasant task — provided that the chosen titles are entertaining enough. The audio tapes of *Harry Potter* also saved our sanity on many a long-distance car trip with our young son and are still snapped into our tape deck, (yes, we do still have one), when the chosen library selection falls short of the required mark. But, and it's an important But, we also have the paper copies of all of the HP series. Somehow to have the actual books, even though every word from them has been superbly read aloud in Stephen Fry's wonderfully adaptive dulcet tones, is still a must. The tape deck could falter, the one in our ancient Berlingo van has already done so, but the paper copies are still sitting happily on my son's old bookshelf upstairs, ready for another generation of readers. So, the audio tape didn't mean the demise of the book-book. It went, rather strangely enough, hand-in-hand. Perhaps though this is something to do with the comfort of being read aloud to?

My son was one of those lucky children who was read to every night and on other occasions too. As many parents know, this can be as pleasurable for the adult as for the child. On a train from Glasgow to Edinburgh when our son was around eight years old, his dad amused him by reading aloud whatever was the current *Harry Potter* volume. Conscious of other passengers, especially of those important looking chaps tapping away on their laptops and blethering into their mobile phones, my husband was thoughtfully keeping his voice low. After ten minutes or so of reading he felt a tap on his shoulder. He groaned inwardly as he waited for the reprimand and request to shut up. Instead the voice said: 'Scuse me, I notice that you have given Hermione a lisp — which is interesting. My voice for her is kind of more like this [....] and can you speak up a wee bit I can't quite hear.'

In Angela MacMillan's edited *A Little, Aloud* (Chatto & Windus, 2010), the introduction notes how listening to someone read can be one of the most profound sources of comfort — a belief many concur with. Somehow, being read to is as if the words curl up and around you, bewitch and cast a spell over us and so remove us from wherever we actually are. We can, of course, be moved into a more scary world depending on the text, but often the very transition of casting the mind out beyond our immediate reality, suspending all that has been rattling around in it all day, is a relief in itself. On the rare occasions when I am too tired to read whatever is my current bedtime book, my husband will read to me and I drift off to sleep lulled by the sound of his voice. And sometimes, while he is reading, my memory store sends up the scent of an old worn wooden desk which is right below my right ear because my head is lying on my folded arms, and I am back in my council estate Primary Five classroom and Mr McPhee is reading aloud *The Hobbit* and I am transfixed.

Apart from reading to our son I have had other experiences of reading aloud. What I have become aware of is that I read best when I read from paper. Recently, at a local artists' evening, I decided at the last minute to change what I had planned to read — the audience didn't feel right for what I had originally chosen. The problem was that the only copy I had of my second choice was on my electronic device. Thinking that words were words were words, I gallantly got up and began to read. As I was on performance mode I gave a rather too enthusiastic swipe to the page in front of me and suddenly found myself reading words which had absolutely no correlation to what I had previously read. I had swooshed on three pages instead of one. I did this a number of times. Each time the audience were patient and respectful when I had to break off and find the correct place. Each time I made a joke of it and I got through the piece. But the swooshing had the effect of fracturing the flow of writing and I made a mental note to stick with paper copy, at least until I had got used to the idiosyncrasies of my wee machine.

Reading aloud is therefore in itself an art form. I think of Marianne Dashwood's annoyance, in *Sense and Sensibility*, when Edward Ferrars reads poetry in, what she judges, a 'spiritless' manner lacking passion, which thus deeply irritates her. When we read a book silently to ourselves, apart from the occasional snort, laugh, murmur, or even tears, we are engaged in an activity that is quite private. When we read aloud the aspect of performance automatically comes into play — even if reading to someone who knows us deeply. We are suddenly conscious of our voice, our distinctive accent, our wariness of how a word should be pronounced, we question if our tone is right, our volume right and a host of other things. In my previous academic existence I had to do quite a bit of reading aloud from different texts. My mind was mostly busy with checking if the passages I had carefully picked out were appropriately illustrating the narrative points that I wanted to get across. But recently, really over the last year or so, I notice that I read in another way. This has perhaps to do with reading out my own work. I know how it goes, I want it to make an impact, so I give it time, I allow for pauses and stresses that I have heard inside my head when I first composed the writing. Without these pauses etc the story doesn't work as I want it to. In doing this I have realised that I need to put aside lurking worries of what listeners may be thinking or why it is that they are fidgeting or staring out of the window. I am learning to block out all of that and pay attention to the words in front of me, for it seems to me that it is only by doing that that the magic will work. Only by doing that will listeners enter the story along with me. And, if done like this, listeners will by-pass my voice and begin to see the images and pictures and movements swirling around behind the words. In other words I need to move beyond being conscious that-I-am-reading and just read. And let the words do all the rest.

Some months ago as part of our book group homework, I read an extract from Edith Nesbit's *The Railway Children* aloud to my husband as it is one of his favourite childhood films. I remember having a little trouble though with Roberta or 'Bobby's' voice as I couldn't get Jenny Agutter's crisp RP out of my mind. It came out as a mix of Scottish Standard English and Valerie Singleton. A few days later I read the short story 'Faith and Hope Go Shopping' by Joanne Harris to all my running gals while on a weekend away. I had taken Angela Macmillan's *A Little, Aloud* with me as I was hopeful of dutifully fulfilling the book group set homework of reading to at least two different people. The running gals and I like to blether and set the world to rights over our shared meals and après-meal, and I didn't want to break into that, but, quite late in the evening when we were all mellow with wine and exercise, I was prompted by one of the runners, who is also in the same book group, to read the story. People did fidget, people did stare out of the window (well, it was a lovely view), people did look as if they were going to sleep (we had run and walked a lot of miles that day), but I soldiered on and gradually there was a real stillness in the caravan. The women seemed to be really listening and I wondered to myself how long it would have been for some of them since they were read to. Afterwards we didn't talk much about the story, instead the reading seemed to act as a means to 'roll up the crumpled skin of the day' as Virginia Woolf so excellently put it, and we all headed for our sleeping bags. Either I had bored them silly or personal memories of being read to as children were uppermost in their minds as, quite soon after I had put the book down, everyone was fast asleep. Would it have mattered if I was reading from an e-book or book-book? Possibly yes, possibly no. In the final analysis, as my Aunt Rachel used to say, perhaps all that really matters is the story.

Scotland, small?

It's getting hard to hold my tongue. I hear Kelvin's voice in my head — 'Don't get involved with a customer's opinions, it's got nothing to do with us'. I do try to follow this advice but there are some subjects that get under my adopted guard. Such as this one. This one which is being lampooned by someone I judge to be totally unqualified to have anything worthy of saying.

'No. It is redeeeculous. Totally redeeeculous. You are too smaaaall. Too insigneeeficant. You have nawthing. Nawthing. You cannot do thees. It is crazee. It makes me lauff.'

I should purse my lips, or at most raise my eyebrows and walk away. It doesn't matter what she thinks. It doesn't matter. It doesn't matter. Only it does. It does to me. So I wade in. Kelvin isn't in the shop at the moment, I am safe from his harrumphing and deliberate asking of me to do some job in another part of the shop.

'So ... the fact that we have always had our own institutions — our own legal system, our own education system, a Kirk over which the present Queen is not the supreme governor as she is in England, and are a small population with valuable energy resources, not to mention our own languages ...'

She interrupts.

'Languages. Plural? Yes, you have Eeengleesh, you have zat strange

Gaaarlic theeng, but zat is not workable for the modern world. It is dead. Gone. Phut!'

I pause momentarily to wonder what Kelvin, being an almost fluent Gaelic speaker might offer as a rejoinder to this — probably just a cutting laugh. I think too of my elder brother whose daily working life is as a Gaelic tutor, running classes in unlikely places as Cumbernauld and Greenock as well as teaching on the popular summer schools in Skye's world famous centre for the fostering of Gaelic language and culture, Sabhal Mòr Ostaig. I could say some of this but as I am aware that I am not up on statistics of how alive the Gaelic tongue really is, so I veer off this track and say instead:

'Well, Scots is alive and kicking in various forms over the country.'

'Scots? Scots? Oh, you mean slang, you mean a bad way of pronouncing theengs.'

Right missus, you've had it.

'Hardly,' I say in my most Miss Jean Brodie tone, 'To begin with, as any serious linguist would tell you, there is no such thing as slang. What you mean by slang is just a name for what is judged as an informal code and therefore not deemed worthy, when in actual fact its internal rules are as complex, if not more so, than Standard English.'

I see her beginning to formulate a response so batter on.

'And Scots is not a lesser form of English. Never has been. Never will be. It has enough distinctive vocabulary to disprove that.

'Geeve me an example,' she says frowning.

'Footerie', 'foosty', 'smeddum', 'wabbit', 'stramash', 'clamjamfrie', 'stravaig'...' I say, picking words out of the air.

'Oh, zey are redeeeculous words. Redeeeculous. Zey are not proper words.'

'They are actually,' I say 'they're Scots'.

'And eef they are, a few leeetle words are not a language.'

'Well, I'm just giving you an example. There are a few more.'

'How many more? Twenty? Feefty? It iz still a redeeeculous argument.'

I hold up my hand. Say, 'Back in a sec', trot round to Scottish Non-Fiction, reach up and take down the weighty paperback tome of the *Concise Scots Dictionary* and return to where she is waiting at Languages.

'Roughly this many,' I say flicking the 817 pages. 'But of course if you want to go further back I advise the on-line resources of what is known as *DOST* — the *Dictionary of the Older Scottish Tongue* — or the more modern listing of the *DSL* — the *Dictionary of the Scottish Language*. Or, what you could do, is simply listen to local people talking.'

She's very slightly nonplussed, but rallies bravely and returns with:

'Oh, I do not come heah very often. I am just veesiting. I am Rrrrussian but I now leeve in London. London is ze only place in theese countree to leeve. The only ceeevilised place.'

I want to say 'Then why by all that is holy, are you wasting my time with your half-baked, prejudiced, ignorant theories, you, you... gowk!'.

But I don't. Of course I don't. As the biblical chaps, chapesses and Pete Seeger would remind us, there is a time to speak your mind and there is a time to be silent. The debate, as far as I am concerned is over. If you're not a resident you don't get a vote. You're not an 'Aye' or a 'Naw' or even a 'Mibby'. Quite frankly, as the voice in my head comments, you've git naething tae dae wi it. Oor time spent payin any heed tae

Londoncentric folk waxing stupidly about oor country which, they have constantly failed to note, runs things a big touch differently, is feenished. Done. We're deciding. Us. Jist us.

So I just smile, code switch to Scottish Standard English — as many Scots have learned to do from knee high — and say 'Having stayed there for a few years in my twenties, and having visited on occasion since, I cannae say I agree. But that's ok. I've my own country. That contents me.'

'You are content wiv heah? Heah? Ver ze rain makes it meeserable all ze time?'

Ah, it's getting silly now. I have things to do and so I smile and as I turn to go, say 'It is a bit soggy at times but it keeps it green and beautiful and anyway, as Billy Connolly has advised, all you need do is get yourself a sexy raincoat and live a little'.

She has the grace to laugh and then suddenly says 'I am Marta. Vot is your name?'

'Anne.'

'Anne. Eet iz goot to meet you. You have speereet. I like zat. I will talk viz you again when I next come.'

'Perhaps we will be an independent country by then.'

'Oh, don't. That ees too funnee. Too funnee!'

And off she goes. Laughing.

We're closing. No, we mean it...

Why is it that some folks can't read signs? And why is it that some folks think that we don't really want to close up at 5.15pm — as the sign says — and go home for our tea? What is it about Cloisters that prompts an assumption that the selling of books is the central priority in the lives of the staff who have no other interests or commitments beyond the shop door? Take for example a vignette played out recently:

5.05pm. It's been a busy day. A bunch of joiners (not sure of the collective noun here…a rachet?) had been battering in the cupboard in the staff corridor for a couple of hours in the morning. The weather had turned thrawn and instead of the projected 'sunny and dry' was 'baltic and sleety'. Having had the shop door propped open to let said joiners trog in and out with miscellaneous bits of wood and other apparent necessary things resulted in the shop becoming a measure more than cold. While they were enjoying themselves with whatever it was they were doing, the window cleaner decided to do what he does (why? it's sleeting!). The chap who comes and takes away our unwanted books had also chosen this morning to call by — hence causing a slight logistical problem in the corridor already overfull of men. And two of our Frequent Flyers had gifted me with their company. The afternoon had been devoid of joiners — well, it was a Friday and you just can't expect folk to work on a Friday afternoon, that's ridiculous — but had been peopled with …em…people. By 5pm I was therefore, quite understandably I think, looking forward to when I could with clear conscience turn the key in the lock, cash up, wash out the coffee things, clear the table, switch off the heaters, the computer, the printer, the cash machine, the router, put the plastic tub out in its usual spot in case of leaking water, get my coat on, gather up the heavy chub lock, put out the lights and go home. I was just wondering if I could perhaps put up the 'Back In 5 Minutes' sign on the door and go and get the dishes done, when the shop door opened.

A youngish man walked slightly unsteadily down to the counter. At first glance I thought he was going to do some sales pitch. He had that look of 'Just been for a wee swally but thoat ah wid see if the folk in the bookshoap would be interested in pittin up ma caird on their noticeboard.' But no. I misjudged. Instead the chap says:

'Scuse me, d'youse hiv any books on poewry? Scawish poewry?'

'Yes, we have some,' I say showing him the section. I can smell alcohol from him and automatically move into a 'Friendly, Helpful, But Not Too Much' mode.

'It's fur ma frien. It's his birthday soon. Ah want tae git him something nice. He's been good tae me. He's a lawyer and dead cliver. Ah first met him...'

'Is he a Burns man, do you know?'I cut in quickly, 'There is a nice four volume set just here. Have a look at them, I've got one or two things to do...'

My hope is that he will peruse them and I can get on with some of the tidy-up. And that will also mean I will avoid what is surely a long drink-nurtured treatise about friendship and how 'Man to man, the world o'er / shall brothers be for a' that.'

'Aye, they look nice. I might take them. See ma friend...'

The shop door jangles and another customer comes in. It's 5.10.

'We're actually closing in a five minutes,' I say.

She ignores me and goes up to the counter.

'Can I help?' I ask as I also arrive there.

'Possibly. I want to order a book on Herodotus.'

Ah Herodotus. That chappy whom the map-maker in *The English Patient* was fond of quoting. You know, him, Fiennes chap who flew Kirsten Scott Thomas over the plains of Africa ... was it Africa or am I confusing Meryl Streep and Robert Redford in *Out of Africa*? I look at the woman before me. Somehow I don't think she would give a jot about the mental image her mention of Herodotus has conjured up. And it is now 5.12.

I also detect a rather odious odour wafting its way around the counter. Ah, a customer with challenges in the cleanliness department. Again, 'Friendly But Not Too Friendly' mode is required. And best get this done quickly.

I punch 'Herodotus' into the computer. As my eye scans down the list of hits, the addled Burns bloke weaves his way back to the counter.

'Whit price did ye say these wur?' he asks.

'Their £40 for the full set but we also have cheaper copies of Burns if you prefer,' I answer not taking my eyes off the screen. I want to finish this and close up.

'£40, that's a lot of money,' says the woman.

'Aye, but see its fur ma good freend. And I've jist earned a wee daud o cash from my painting and decorating joab,' returns the chap.

'Oh, I need a painter and decorator!' she exclaims.

'Dae ye? Well, ah'm yer man. Nooo, I've hid a wee drink, jist cause it's Friday, but ah'm always sober when on the joab. Whit de ye need paintin?' he enquires propping his elbow on the counter, settling in for a good chat.

'There only seems to be something called *Herodotus, Book VIII* listed, is that any good?' I quickly interject.

'No. I want *Herodotus II*. Well, it's the stairwell in my close, really a disgrace it is…' and off she goes describing the state of her walls much to the avid interest of her slightly swaying audience.

'So you want *The History of Herodotus, Book II* ?' I ask.

'Yes,' she says snippily.

Right, time to close this deal.

'In that case there isn't anything listed. I think you will need to come back in a week or so and maybe there will be something then.'

Really. Enough. It's now 5.15.

'No, I'll just ask Norman. He will know where to get it. He knows all these things. He told me to read it. He also thinks my stairwell is a disgrace. You know the other day, I …'

There are two customers politely waiting behind the scented woman. Standing, I note, about a yard back. Hopefully not downwind.

'Will I take your books?' I ask.

The first chap stretches out to hand his over. The woman doesn't move to let him nearer to counter. She seems oblivious. Herodotus II and her stairwell are far more important than other mere mortals.

I swiftly ring up the books of both men. They give me the exact money. Refuse a bag and dart to the door. I guess they can only hold their breath for so long.

The Burns chap is now on to colour schemes.

'Ah, kin dae ye a nice cerise colour. Dead classy it is. Every yin likes it. Or mibby ...'

'Sorry folks, I need to close up now, maybe you could come back in tomorrow or whenever you have more time.'

I step out from the counter and walk up to the door. Put out a set of lights. That seems to waken them a bit.

'Oh, are you closing?' says the fragrant woman.

'Yes, sorry, I am,' I say. The fewer words the better.

'So, as I say, the cerise is nice but ...'

I move back down to the counter. At least they have both now turned in the direction of the door. I switch into a past life secondary teacher body stance, smile but wave them both down the aisle to the door saying firmly:

'Bye then. Thanks for coming in.'

They saunter down to the door. I rush ahead, pull it open. They amble over the threshold and come to a dead stop just inside the storm doors. Doesn't matter, I can barricade myself in with just the inside door. As I turn the lock I hear her say 'I will need to ask the neighbours if they will put up some money, do you know what one of them said last week...'

I leave them to it. Hurtle around the shop tidying, sorting, reckoning, switching. Get my coat on, grab the big lock, switch off the last light, pull open the door. They are still there.

'... no really, you wouldn't credit the behaviour of some people.'

'But you could always go for the Burnt Sienna, that's quite popular too. I think I've goat a wee photie of a wall I used it fur recently.'

'Sorry, folks, could you just step out of the doorway, so I can lock up,' I ask.

They step out four steps and carry on talking. Neither listening to the other.

I secure the heavy storm doors, plug in the lock, shoot the bolt, turn the key, drop it in my bag and turn homewards. It's 5.30pm.

The Meek Should Inherit

He reminds me of the type of chap that the late, lamented and unique singer/songwriter, Michael Marra, sung about in his wonderful song 'Hermless' which espouses the virtues of simplicity, quietness, modesty and douceness. It is what eco folk would call living lightly on the earth. What zen masters recognise as the mindful practice of drawing water from the well and chopping wood. What Thoreau identified as a life 'lived deliberately', stripped of complexity and extraneous baggage. All of these praxes are what makes up the daily doings of Mr MacDonald (no, not the literal hewing of wood — duh — that was just a useful metaphor). He's one of our Frequent Flyers but he's in the undemanding category. The great interest in his life is football and the collation of football programmes, football stats, football DVDs. Is this baggage? Is it unnecessary? Possibly, but I get the feeling that there will come a day when he will decide that he doesn't need any of it and offer his vast collection to the first interested person he meets. He has you see what the Buddhist would know as detachment. The picking up, the holding of, the usage of something, then the putting down, the returning, the letting go for someone else to do the same. That's what makes him a born library user. He gets the principle. It makes sense to him. And he still has faith in the system.

A favourite saying of Mr MacDonald's is: 'I'll probably get it in the library.' Whether that holds true these days and whether Mr MacDonald's belief in libraries is merited, is highly and sadly debatable.

The large library in our town was gifted to the people of the town by a prosperous local thread mill manufacturer in 1871 and extended in 1904. The books were donated by the town's philosophical society and other generous donors. In the inaugural opening a guest speaker enthused that 'a great want is no doubt being supplied by the establishment of this institution, and you may look forward to the moral and intellectual elevation of the community at large…' What, one wonders, would these same philanthropic folk think of the current praxis of down-scaling not just the holdings of public libraries across the country but indeed of the actual existence of libraries themselves? As we frequently experience in Cloisters, not everyone has access to the Internet, and even if they have, are not always desirous of buying a book. Sometimes they simply want to have a look at it, check or gain some information of varying genres or perhaps enjoy a story, an account, a poem or a play and then … put it back. And not all of this is available on the Internet. And bookshops need to sell books to survive. So this is where libraries come in. Or should come in.

I was one of those fortunate children who was taken to our local library every Saturday afternoon when possible. I loved going there. Our library was situated in an old manor house in a park. Even the walk there was nice and we had the added pleasure of a swing or a shot on the roundabout as we trundled through the park. Once inside the library, a whole world was opened up — and all for free! My mum would leave us to batter up the stairs to the children's library while she had no doubt a very welcome half hour of peace in the adult's section. We would descend some while later, clutching a swag of books, stamped and dated by the lady who had told us to 'Wheesht!' if we got too excited during our excavations. We would then walk the long road home to our Scottish Special housing scheme which had been built on the periphery of the town — so as to keep the 'real' townsfolk uncontaminated by these 'Glasgow Overspill' lesser beings — and then very happily slump down for a good read of our weekly cache. My favourite place was behind the living-room couch. I guess, being one of four kids, it offered a semi-solitary place where I could focus on my book instead of getting drawn into other pursuits. Or maybe it was that I was just securing the best defensive position for when the mutant Daleks appeared on our telly a bit later. But whatever the reason, I thought it quite magical that you could go to a place full of books, pick out something that looked good, find others by that same person, show them to the woman behind the desk and then get to take them home for three whole weeks if you wanted.

It wasn't until much later that I discovered that this same library also had a room called 'Reference Section' which had books that you couldn't take home but you could sit and read there and then. This mystery was unlocked for me when I was in my last year of secondary schooling when, now a sixth year pupil with spaces on her timetable and needing some help with something called 'Research' for my Sixth Year Studies English topic of the 'Social Comment in Selected Novels of Dickens', I wandered down to our library which was conveniently situated very near my school. The librarian, realising I was after what I would now know as 'critique of Dickens' or 'the metalanguage around his writing', showed me the Reference Room. And I found my second home. Rows of books talking about stuff that was useful, chairs and desks to read the stuff and quiet, lovely quiet.

I was fortunate to find this room, fortunate to then go on and find many such rooms, many such helpful librarians, and perhaps fortunate to know them before the arrival of the computer. I am writing this on my iMac at home — the room I am in has a large wall of shelved books, I am sitting at a desk, and apart from a dog wandering in now and again, it is quiet. It is in some ways my very own reference library. And I have the Internet. I have already checked it a couple of times for a snippet of information but I have also checked two or three real books and a journal too. Despite my own large personal collection and despite the ease of access to the Internet, now and again I come across a title — yes, it really is true — that is not digitally available. This is where I need a library. A good library. Not just one that stocks the latest James Patterson or Lee Child — entertaining though their writing is. And until every book of erudition is scanned and made available for fortunate folk like me who have the technology to access it, I need the libraries of Scotland, of the British Isles and other parts of the world, to hold and steward those books. Not sell them off or chuck 'em out. And I am afraid, dear appalled reader, this is exactly what happened in our local library along the road from Cloisters. Someone, working from some obscure understanding of education for the masses, decided that the reference section (gifted to the people of the town remember), was obsolete and under-used. And a major cull happened. Books that are irreplaceable were loaded up onto trestle tables and sold off and the remainder boxed up and given to a charity. The argument, I suppose, was that the townspeople weren't regularly reading the books which took up a huge amount of shelf space. But this argument has the obvious flaw in that we cannot say what future researchers will be looking for and what piece of history has now been lost. The other thing was that no-one thought to approach Kelvin and ask, as the only existing bookseller in the town whose stock is vastly different than that of WH Smith or The Works, if he would like first chance to buy some of the more rare titles. As it was he got wind of what was happening, went along and bought some of the books. But the point here is not who managed to buy what, who bagged a bargain, but the cool hand decision to move on from books in favour of the computer. As Jeannette Winterson has commented, libraries have shifted from places of learning with helpful people who know about books, to community centres with books. I should quickly say this is not the fault of the serious librarian. No, 'tis the result of stupidity elsewhere. When someone out of work and claiming benefit is told the only way they can keep claiming benefit is to demonstrate that they have applied for X amount of jobs per week, then they have to use the Internet to find those adverts for those jobs. If you don't have your own computer — many still do not despite what government officials may think — then the obvious place to go is the library. The library has always been the starting point for help, but whereas it was at one time the starting point for help with books, it is now the starting point for access to on-line information. And the poor librarians, trained in the Dewey system and other classifications, now find themselves the butt of exasperation by the public who have to wait in line for their turn on the computer. A friend of mine commented recently that the job of a local librarian these days is a fusion of community and social worker, with a bit of book knowledge thrown in.

Ok, so this is bit of a rant. But I think it a rant worth the ranting. We need to defend our libraries for people like our nice Mr MacDonald who doesn't have his own computer, isn't, I think, interested in getting one, and, besides all of that, enjoys going to the library. And his belief in the library deserves to be merited. I notice too that where others may groan about the library catalogue system being temporarily inactive (probably due to some essential upgrade going on behind the scenes), Mr MacDonald will stoutly defend this by saying 'The librarian couldn't check my book out in the usual way this morning, but I'm sure they'll get it sorted.' And anyway, the bottom line is that I am a fan of Mr MacDonald because, with the grace of a gentleman, he requested my last book at our local library, read it, even though he never reads anything outside of the football world, or indeed outside of facts and figures, came into the bookshop specifically to tell me that he had read it and that the library had told him to return it quickly as it had a waiting list. Why should I not like this man? Why should I not defend libraries, especially if they stock my book?

Trust in Allah but tie up your camel

It's a minute to quarter past ten. I slip my key into the big chub lock, my mind plunging forward to what I need to do once inside. I usually try to get to the shop earlier so to do the opening-up routine in peace but I've been enjoying a blether with the two women who work in the fruit and veg shop opposite. They are a mother and daughter set-up and to my mind constitute a great team. Despite having had to get up at 5am even in the horrible dark winter mornings, and despite the fact that their shop has no door but only a pull up-and-down metal security shield which means they have to wear around twenty layers of clothing, they are always bright and chatty. And the shop is good — boxes of fresh fruit and veg stacked floor to ceiling, all neatly arranged, all tempting. I tend to limit myself to the bananas, the succulent strawbs when in season and the big packets of spinach. I keep promising myself I will investigate the stock more but as, like today, I should really be already in the bookshop, I prefer to spend the time in a few minutes chat. We tend to focus on what the weather is doing, if we managed to get some washing out and why is it that men just don't notice a clarty house. That last one could keep us going for a few hours. The talk did turn to books though as Kelvin had managed to track down and promptly deliver a volume that the women were interested in — I judge that good community relations. As I have already delineated, the area is a struggling one and it's important that all the shop folk foster a sense of camaraderie. One never knows when the safe port of nearby shop, where the bookshop staff are known, could be more than useful.

So, anyway, I'm now slightly late and focussing on getting myself on the other side of the door and doing the Switch On, I don't notice the chap walking up to me or pay attention to what he is saying.

'Hen. Hen. Did ye hear whit ah said?'

I've got as far as opening the first storm door and am reaching up for the top lock when I register that he's talking to me.

'Sorry. What did you say?'

'Ah said, there's a bunch of books lying jist in that close door. Look, there. C'mere till ah show ye.'

I'd prefer to get on with what I should be doing but it might be wise to acquiesce.

I walk with him a few steps down the street. At the grubby close entrance, the same close that the bookshop backs on to, is a large plastic bag with some old books spilling out of it.

'See. There's a Burns. Somebuddy must hae left them fur ye.'

I wonder if that's true. The close offers more shelter than our shop door and they are obviously books …

'Ah'll help ye cairry them in,' says the chap.

I scan the street. There doesn't seem to be anyone running towards us yelling to leave their books alone.

'Um. Ok. I can always leave them just inside our door and see if anyone comes back for them.'

'Och, they'll no come back. They must be fur youse.'

He lifts up the bulky bag, waits patiently while I get the inside door open and dumps it down just inside.

'There ye go. Ah hope ye git a good price fur them. See ye then.'

I leave the bag where it is and gallop up the shop. It's now almost 10.20. Things to do. Things to do.

I've just managed to get all the lights on, the till on, the computer on when the shop door opens. A wee man appears — the type of man who immediately activates my caw canny instinct. He's scruffy. That's no crime, but it's the type of scruffiness that suggests he may need to take advantage of any opportunity for getting money. He comes nearer the counter, close enough for me to see his eyes. They're clear. No drugs or alcohol there — at least at the moment. I also see his wide grin, his weather-beaten, lined but open face.

'Good morning Sir. Can I help?'

'I'm glad you're open. I came by earlier but ye were shut. Ah just wondered if ye would be interested in ma books.'

He's carrying a battered and less-than-clean shoulder bag which he hitches up onto the counter.

'Ah had more but someone's away wi them.'

I point up towards the shop door where the bag of books is lying.

'Those?'

'Aye! Aye! Hey, that's great. Here am thinking that it wis ma win fault fur leaving them and here some good angel has lifted them and brought them here. Wis it you?'

'No, someone else saw them and brought them here. I'm glad you came in.'

'So am ah. See, that just shows ye. Ye need tae trust. The universe is looking aifter ye even when ye don't think it. And ma karma is guid. The universe knows that.'

Judging by his appearance and obvious lack of ready cash, or perhaps even a regular place to lay his head, I wonder about the laws of karma, but he seems quite content with them.

'And are you hoping to sell these or are you just handing them in?'

'Ah could really dae wi a wee bit money tae get a power card. Anything ye can dae hen wid be appreciated.'

Having stolen his books I guess I do owe him something. I should probably say that his we're not taking in books at the moment — as the sign on the door informs — but …

'Let's see what you've got then.'

He empties his manky bag out. An ancient atlas, gritty, water damaged and bevelled. Three volumes of a History of the English language — which we already have in better condition. The volumes are passable though.

'Ah'll get the others,' he says.

The others turn out to be a Collins edition of Burns, grungy with some crumpled pages and two old dictionaries. The best place for most of these is the recycle box.

'They were ma dad's. I've kept them aw these years. But it's time tae let them go. And ma dad widnae deny me a wee bit electricity if he could.'

Ach, dearie me. I should say no thanks. I shouldn't encourage this kind of thing. I know that. Kelvin wouldn't take them. Or would he? There's a kind heart very near the surface of his skin. Och, whit the hell. My karma could do with a boost. And if Kelvin objects I'll pay the money myself.

'I shouldn't take them. The boss has asked us not to. But I did take your books and cause you worry. So, just this time, and really just this time, how about a fiver?'

'Aw hen, you really are an angel. A fiver wid do me just nice. Bless ye. See, that's a guid lesson fur me. A lesson in trust. Ah believe in aw that. Trust that the right thing'll happen. Trust that there's guid folk aroon ye. Although ah hiv tae say I prefer the wisdom of the Arabs.'

'What's that?'

'Trust in Allah, but tie up your camel.'

'Ah, wise words. Wise words, specially round these parts.'

'Right ah need tae git up the road. Cheeriebye hen.'

'Bye Sir. Have a good day.'

'Ah will. Oh, ah will.'

I watch him go. His open beaming smile looms in my mind. A happy man. He has little but doesn't care. Content to float along on the wash of life. Was that some kind of karmic test? And did I pass or fail?

Atonement

I come out of the Staff corridor on my way towards the table where I had been cleaning books bound for Music.

'Jings Almighty!' goes my inner voice.

Sitting at the table is what I think is a massive gnome. A very still and staring gnome. Looking as if he has always sat there. Completely impassive like a cardboard cut-out.

Realigning my shaken veins I take a couple of steps towards the table hoping our visitor hadn't seen me jump. Hoping that he is just a product of the incredibly hot weather we have been having for the last few days which has played havoc with hydration levels.

'Hallo,' I say, partly to follow bookshop etiquette but more than anything to test if he is real.

'Hallo,' he replies. 'Just reading. Just reading the books.'

'That's ok,' I say.

It's difficult to decide what age he is. Anything from sixteen to thirty-six might cover it. And, not meaning to be cruel, but he has the most enormous face I have ever seen. It seems to balloon out from his shoulders and is as broad as it is long. And, to complete the look, he has a wee woolly hat perched in Smurf fashion on the top of his head. From what I can see, the rest of him looks pretty massive too.

I look at the books in front of him. Books I had left on the table all bound for Children Non-Fiction. Interesting but surely way too young for him. I wonder if he didn't want to presume that he would be allowed to look at others.

'I'm waiting for my pal. His wife says he's not in till 1pm. I'm just waiting here. I don't want to wait there.'

'That's fine,' I say. 'Feel free to look at other books if you want.'

'I don't like waiting there. She's ... well, she's ok but ...', he grimaces.

'Not your kind of person?' I prompt

'No,' he says and relaxes his face into a sheepish grin.

'Would you like some coffee while you wait?'

'It's Ramadan,' he says 'but thanks all the same.'

There's something about the latter half of his sentence that reassures me. The balance of body mass and intellect may be out of sync but his politeness levels are just fine.

'How's that going for you?' I ask.

'S'alright,' he says.

'Must be difficult though eh? Not being able to eat or drink till nightfall — which in Scotland at this time of year isn't till around 10.30. Seems a bit unfair to me.'

'Yeh, but s'alright,' he says again, loyal to his creed. 'I've to go back to my pal's at 1pm, will you tell me when that is?'

I look at the clock on the wall. It's only 11.45am. Oh dear.

'Can you order me a book?' he says suddenly.

'Sure. What book?'

'Any book. Any book.'

'Um … we would need a title.'

'I don't mind.'

'Well, there's quite a lot of books out there. It would be better if you chose one.'

'*Eastenders*,' he says after a minute.

'We should have something on *Eastenders* in the shop itself,' I say.

I go up to Film and Media. Sure enough there is an old annual based on the show a few years ago. I take it back to him.

He smiles and begins to turn the pages. I leave him to it.

A few minutes later he asks 'Can I order another one of these?'

'Eh, the same one? or a different one?'

'Same one.'

I wonder if he needs things explaining a bit.

'Do you understand that this is a bookshop? You can buy books here. We're not a library. But we can also order books for you if they are not in the shop.'

'Yes, order a book,' he says. 'Same one'.

'Kelvin,' I call 'Could you perhaps deal with this gentleman's order?'

Kelvin had snuck into the seat at the till while this interchange was going on. He's skilled at dealing with people whose thought processes don't quite run on usual lines. He remains unflustered and patient until the desired title and order has been achieved. This is most certainly a virtue but the undoubted side effect is that people, who may not find such forbearance elsewhere, tend to perceive the bookshop as a place they will not be hurried out of, and we therefore have to deal with the consequences of that. But in such acceptance is the uniqueness of Cloisters contained. I doubt I would be writing this book were it 'a proper shop' as Kelvin often says.

I leave them to it and move up to Music with the cleaned books. More customers come in. More happenings happen. An hour goes by. I forget about the gnomish chap as I work steadily on. The shop door jangles. He appears again. I hadn't seen him leave which is surprising considering his bulk.

'Still not in,' he says and makes his way back to the table. 'She said to try later. She's alright but …'

I suspect the whole script is about to be repeated. I let him wander down to the table. Finish what I was doing and decide to take a lunch break. The shining sun is well up and it just feels wise to absent myself for a half hour.

Ten minutes later sitting in a shady corner of a hidden strip of garden in the grounds of the local university, my bare feet enjoying the cool grass, my lunch of water, cherry tomatoes, humous, pitta bread and strawberries spread out before me, (the perfect repast for a hot hot day), I find myself thinking about the chap. On initial contact my whole being wanted to select the 'Avoid' option. I count myself as having a good measure of compassion for other beings, I think I am kind, I think I am (mostly) tolerant — but this self diagnosis is obviously put into jeopardy when I sniff the high possibility of yet another frequenter of the bookshop who will need special handling. Where my lower self groans and thinks 'Oh good grief, not another one!' my higher self counteracts this by suggesting that if I were the mother of such a son, unsure in mind and body, who probably experiences rejection wherever he goes, I would be so grateful for somewhere that accepts him just as he is. It is Ramadan after all. I'm not Muslim and don't ever expect to be, but I get the concept of the attempt to counter past sins, the purging of selfish excess and non-caring attitudes, and the endeavour to remain humble. Despite all his lumbering difficulties and his non-comprehension that three hours in an independent bookshop is probably a tad too long, in his favour is that he has managed to retain a politeness, a hesitation of speaking badly of others — 'She's alright' — and a patience with us who think we are so perfect. And he has, I think, ordered a book. If he is still in the bookshop when I get back, I may smile at him.

Once a Mill Girl

A little lady is dancing in front of me. Lifting her arms and dropping them in a smooth repetitive movement. Sashaying her hips and singing. She's not here, she's away back in time at her machine. Working and singing. Working and singing.

Que sera, sera / Whatever will be, will be / the future's not ours to see…

Her shopping bags lie forgotten at her feet. They're unimportant. Not part of her reverie. She ends the refrain 'Que sera, seraaaaaa….' and comes to a stop, her casual black loafers clump down on the carpet, her arms return to her side, her eyes refocus.

'Aye. That's what we did. That's what we did.'

'You enjoyed your time in the mills then?'

'Oh aye. Aye. It wis hard sometimes but ah enjoyed it. Ah miss it sometimes. But ah hiv ma memories. They keep me gaun. And I'll enjoy this. Mibby I'll know somebuddy in it.'

She taps her ringed finger on a slim A4 book lying on the counter. It's Evelyn Hood's *Mill Memories* published some years ago, which we have recently begun to stock. And it's proving popular. This wee lady had spied the copy in the window and it drew her into the bookshop, a place she had never been.

'Ah'm glad ah came in here,' she says 'ah'm no a great reader, but ah'll read this. And thanks fur listening tae me hen. It's no everyone that wid dae that.'

'I'm interested in the mills,' I say 'It's fascinating history. I like to know the history of wherever I live. And this town has a great history.'

'Aye, it dis,' she says 'we need tae be mair proud of it and get the cooncil tae dae mair aboot preservin it.'

'I believe there's an extension to the museum planned that will celebrate the textile industry of the town,' I offer.

'Ah hope that happens, ah really do. We deserve it.'

We blether a bit more about the mills and the shame of many of the old buildings being destroyed or left to ruin, but agree that those left standing are fine looking testaments. It strikes me though that like so many of the former mill workers I have spoken with, their knowledge of their place of work rests more on their personal involvement, the fun, the mutual trust, the many friendships, the feeling of identity, belonging and security of work. The actual origins and historical trajectory of the mills isn't something that is deeply known about. For many of the workers the mills were the people in them, not the building. Perhaps that's a facet of human nature, if the heart is happy it can exist quite cheerfully in whatever surrounding.

Cheer is something the former mill girls seem to have in abundance. That was certainly my experience when, for purposes of research for a clutch of poems I had been asked to write, I had the privilege of interviewing some women who had spent many years in the mills. I worried a little if my questions would be structured enough so as to open up a shy speaker perhaps not used to being recorded. I need not have worried. Their thoughts and memories about their time in the mills came spilling out of the women in language that was vibrant, detailed and alive. I listened and prayed that the technology on my mobile phone was capturing it all. When I got home later, my head still ringing with the sound of the women's voices, the following poem more or less wrote itself:

IN MA DAY
A prose poem for Annie, Isa, Jessie, Jean and Nancy

In ma day
in the Rewinding
we were given overalls.
Green, wrap-over, short-sleeved,
tied at the side.
One fur washin, one fur wearin.
But ye werena allowed tae cut them.
So me, being sae wee, had tae tack up a hem aboot ten inches.
At least ah always got ma ain back
when they took them away fur launderin.

In ma day
in the Twining
ye wore baffies.
Comfy, loose weave, hessian slippers,
that kept yer feet cool.
Shoes were too hot. It wis aye hot.
But ye didnae wear them ootside.
An ye pit yer hair into a net
or a turban to stop it catchin
or getting messed up.

In ma day
the first thing ye learned wis the weaver's knot.
Ah can still dae it in ma sleep.
Ye were issued wi a wee pair o scissors
and shown how tae hold them wi yer pinkie.
But ah wisnae allowed tae use ma ain spring scissors
which were dead quick.
And ah mind the wee brushes
'cap bar nebs' we cawd them
as we went along cleaning them.

In ma day
ye went tae the mills because it wis a guid job.
Left the school on the Friday, startit on the Monday.
£3.12 shillings a week then on to piece work.
Ma mither and her mither worked there afore me
but they worked in their bare feet,
stoppin the spindles wi their big toe.
A manager asked me wance if I could do it
an ah did.

In ma day
us in Ferguslie
were cawd the Mill Hairies.
They said we wur tough.
Ah don't sae much know if we wur.
Mibby we jist sounded it.
But we cawd the posh wans and them in Embroidery
'The Lady Buddies'.
Ah'm no saying they didnae wurk. They did.
It wis just different from oors.

In ma day
we jist pit up wi the noise. Aw the noise!
Nae wunner ah still talk so loud.
They didnae think o ear plugs till much later.
But they wur guid in other ways.
Gave out orange juice when it wis too hot,
offered a saving scheme
a guid pension, holidays,
maybe a chance tae be a teacher
or a forewummin.

In ma day
when the shift ended
droves of wummin wid run fur the buses aw lined up.
Annie though, she'd a system gaun wi her mither.
They'd swap her wee girl atween them at the gate
so she was aye looked aifter.
But us single girls wid cleek airms

and walk thegither up tae King Street
fur a hot pie.
Jist a pie. But it wis great somehow.

In ma day
yer mither gave ye a big pin
tae clip yer weekly pay poke ontae ye
so to bring it hame tae her safe.
The money wis needit.
But sometimes I took a wee bit oot o it
An made up a story of why ah was short.
Ah still feel guilty from that.
But ah wis young an
wantit some fun sometimes.

In ma day
ye were brought up tae help folk.
But it got me intae trouble.
Ah wis young and did ma wurk fast.
So then ah wid help the older wummin.
The foreman didnae like this.
Dae yer ain wurk! he wid say.
Ah says it wisnae any o his business if ah wantit tae help folk.
He didnae like me back-chattin, so ah git pit tae No.9
And here, ah wis teamed up wi aulder wummin again!

In ma day.
they said ah wid like it at the Finishing mill
but ah didnae.
Fur fourteen year ah did
shifts o eight hours
6 till 2 or 2 till 10
Wan hour fur yer lunch an
ye hid tae clean yer machine,
run away doon tae Mile End fur yer dinner
an away back up aw they stairs again.
Four flights.
The lift wasnae very safe.
Slurp yer tea from the trolley
without stopping your wurk your wurk your wurk

In ma day
we hid some right laughs.
Me an aw the others.
Always some cairry-on going on.
They couldnae stop ye.
Neither could they stop ye singin.
We sang aw the songs. It kept ye gaun.
But wee May wid shout: Ah hope thae ends are aw up!
Ah hope they ends are aw up!

In ma day
if yer frame went wrang ye went tae the toilets
fur a good greet.
Someone wid always come in and tell ye no tae mind.
And Jessie wis great at daein yer hair
– pittin it in rollers on a Friday afternoon
An ye got yer ears pierced in the toilets an aw
using a raw tawtie and a bit o string pit through the hole.
Ah didn't dae it though.

In ma day
they looked aifter ye
A nurse, chiropodist an dentist to hand.
An the dinner hall did great food
Three courses.
The lassie wi the lisp that got excited
about 'roast n rice n prunes the morra' still makes me laugh.
An if ye spotit Miss Reel on the Summer Rothesay trip ye got money.
But it wis only me that realised it was the wee mousey girl.

In ma day
a lot of us met oor man through the mills
or at the dances.
We girls wid practise the steps in the toilets
watching oor reflection in the shiny green tiled walls.
But if ye fancied fresh air there wis the bowlin and Rec club
where we played everythin but fitba.
Aye. Ah wid hiv worked on if they wid hiv let me.
But they didnae.

Today
people say Coatses gifted the toon
wi aw they big grand buildings
– the church, the toon hall, the observatory,
Fountain Gardens and whitever else.
But it wisnae them. It wis us! We did that.
Us that stood aw they hours in front o a machine.
Us that liftit they heavy cheeses, transferred they cones an pushed
they bogeys.
Us that got groin strains, varicose veins an lopsided hips
frae whit we had tae dae.
Us that pit this toon on the map.
Us. Us. Us.
In ma day.

This poem formed part of a specially organised event in the local thread mill museum — a volunteer run organisation which courageously holds safe the story of the town's mills. The women I had interviewed for my poem all came along to this special event, dressed up in what they would have worn when working. And, true to the famous zest of the mill girls, added their own distinctive contribution — dancing and singing (even the ninety one year old who took great joy in demonstrating her ability to still do high kicks), surprising and delighting the audience who had wondered if they were in for a dreary time of endless poetry. When I read out the poem above, in as close a tone as had been said to me, I looked up at one point to see how it was being received by the women that had shared their memories. Two of them had tears in their eyes, others nudged each other when they heard their particular memory read out and, as I reached the final lines, 'But it wisnae them. It wis us! We did that…' the women whooped and cheered. It was my turn to feel tears in my eyes.

I was not born nor bred in this town but, having now lived here for over two decades, I feel blessed to share in its history, its spirit, its distinct mix. There is much that is wrong in the town, but there is much that is right. The continuing verve of the former mill girl, still living in the heart and bones of many of its older residents, is most definitely one of the rights.

Hot Books

Spiritual gurus have, since writing began, sought to warn us that what we think is permanent is impermanent and that change is inevitable. But it is only when we see this in action that we understand the (ironically) definitive nature of the teaching. I felt the impact of this one Sunday evening when my son strolled into our living room asking:

'Ma, what street is the bookshop on?'

'Corner of Valley and Water Street, why?'

'You might want to check your email. I've sent you something.'

'Sent something?'

'Yeh, better check it out.'

There was something in his tone that had me skipping into our dining room where my computer lives. I logged on, tapped on the email icon and scrolled to find the latest emails. The most recent was a forwarded message entitled 'Inferno Wrecks Shops and Flats'. Attached to it was a photo depicting fire crews, numerous fire engines, a sprawling spaghetti of hose pipes, extended cranes, and lots of grey smoke. The street, or what was discernible of it, was a west facing shot of Valley Street just before it meets Water Street. The focus of the fire services attention appeared to be on a shop around fifty metres east of the bookshop and on the other side of the street. Oh, phew! But heck, this is a serious incident. I checked my phone — no message from Kelvin. Either he was was down there with his hard hat drenching down the outside of the shop and making plans to evacuate the best of the thousands of books, or he was at home throwing scornful comments at the telly in blissful ignorance. I guessed, or hoped, it would be the latter and so simply forwarded the email to him. Two minutes later he replied asking 'Which shop is that?' So that was fine. If the Police hadn't alerted him then they didn't deem Cloisters to be in any danger.

Travelling to the bookshop the next morning I was curious as to what evidence there would be of the fire. I had taken the car as I wanted to get home quickly after lock-up so to get to a friend's house for a road run — training for the local 10k which was fast looming. As I came near the end of town where the bookshop resides, I noted that one of the usual access streets had blue Police tape stretched over it and a large sign advising of some street closures and the diversion route in place. I wondered if I would have to find a different parking place from that of my norm but the diversion route took me into Water Street and I parked the car in the usual side street. Valley Street was totally closed to all traffic — but, bizarrely, busier than I had ever seen it. The owners of the supermarket opposite the burnt out building were standing chatting with a group of people, all gesticulating and nodding towards the charred and empty space that had once been a shop and four residential flats. In my three years of working in Cloisters I have never seen the supermarket closed. Never. There was another ten minutes to our opening time so, unwilling to miss out on any low-down on the fire, I scooted over to the fruit and veg shop.

My favourite staff were on duty and were already deep in conversazione with a local. It was one of those times where it was totally legit to put your elbow on the counter and get stuck in.

'Morning folks. Some fire eh?'

'That's whit we're just saying. Terrible isn't it. Just terrible. Those poor folk.'

'Do we know how it started?'

'No. No yit. But we're jist saying, it couldnae hiv been a torch job 'cos ye widnae take the chance of being done fur murder, 'cos that's what could hiv happened. So it must hiv been an accident.'

'At least no-one was hurt.'

'Aye. Thank God. No-one. That's the main thing.'

'That's it. But those poor folk in the flats above. They must hiv got a right fright. And some wee kiddies too. But they're all ok. They were taken to the Braes Hotel. Lost everything though that's the thing. Everything. Ye canna imagine that.'

We all nod. And it's true, none of us can imagine it.

Time was ticking on and, as there didn't seem to be anymore goss to be had, I said goodbye and ran back over to the bookshop.

There were three Police cars parked in collision fashion just outside of the shop. No need today to feel any niggling worries about security. The boys are all here.

I get on with opening up and switching on. Am just parcelling up some Amazon books when the door jangles and a fireman comes in. In that he doesn't have his headgear or breathing apparatus on I guess that this isn't an emergency visit, but perhaps more of a check that the bookshop is ok. Turns out to be none of that.

'Don't panic,' he grins 'Just want to take a wee swatch at a book in your windae.'

'Would you like some coffee while your swatching?' I ask in the hope of gleaning some inside info.

'Naw thanks, somebuddy's just brought us a flask.'

I could argue that our coffee will be far nicer but think that that could sound a bit desperate. Better not. I could maybe still get some detail though. But, just as I finish the final Amazon book and begin to move up the shop to the window display, he shuts the graphic novel he was perusing and moves towards the door.

'Need to go. Thanks hen.'

And off he goes. Damn. Wasn't quick enough.

The morning moves on. Various customers appear. None of whom I recognise. A number of them say something like:

'I jist took a wee stroll up to see what had happened wi that fire and then saw your shop. Are youse ok?'

And then, after a quick scan of the shelves and shelves of books:

'Load of books in here eh? Just as weel it wisnae youse — aw this paper, that wid make a right blaze.'

Have to say that thought had crossed my mind.

The day rumbles on. The street remains busy with diverted traffic, with buses full of people craning their necks to see the remaining rubble that is the destroyed building, with uniformed and suited men, and curious sight-seers.

Everyone who comes into Cloisters talks of the fire. Kelvin will be sorry he has missed all the buzz as he is away on a planned walk. Some of the regulars joke that it is highly suspicious that no-one knows how the fire started but the bookshop owner is nowhere to be seen. Desmond says that his worst nightmare is that the bookshop goes on fire. I say that at least it would save us battling with the swamping yardage of books everyday. He says that that is a terrible thing to say and I should be ashamed. I say that you have to work in a second-hand bookshop to understand. He says it makes him feel sick to think of anything happening to the bookshop. I decide not to pursue the subject.

But despite the curious buzz and strange sense of excitement in the street it is still sad that four families and a shopkeeper have lost so much. I think of what it must be like to have to suddenly evacuate your home, seeing flames lick at your door, grabbing bare essentials — such as beloved people, pets, your wallet? a coat? It must have been a scary scene as, according to the supermarket owner whom I spoke to later in the afternoon, there were some wee children out on the street in their bare feet having been lifted to safety by the fire crew.

Half an hour before closing time a woman comes in asking for Martina Cole books. I show her some titles, she selects some and brings them to the counter. And of course we talk about the fire. She tells me that there are already two collection points designated for donations of clothing and toiletries and other basics for the homeless families.

'They say there wis two weans standing out on the street wi no shoes, puir lambs. And one of the families had a wee baby just two months auld. They've nothing left. Nothing. They're all ok. But still. Nothing. Canna imagine it can ye? So if ye want tae donate anything ye can hand it in tae any o the two centres. I'm gonnae dae that the morra. And there wis a dug tae. So somebuddy's already given in some food for him. Well, it's the least ye can dae isn't it?'

There are so many terrible things happening in the world. At the time of writing, hell is ruling in Gaza, children are dying, people are in desperate need. And that is only one place of terror and conflict. There are so many. But here, in our town, people are organising to help four families who are in need. Just four families. Yes, there are many others possibly in need too, and maybe there's a bit of sensationalism attached to this one — but that's a cynic's point of view. The truth of the matter is that local people want to help right and soothe a situation, do some good, hold out a helping hand. I'm glad the bookshop is in this town.

The Resolution

It is time to stop writing. Yesterday one of our Frequent Flyers asked me to call him by his first name.

'All this Mr this and Mr that, it's too formal, just call me James, I've been coming here long enough,' he asserted.

I didn't want to call him James. I don't want to call him James because if I do that it means that I am no longer on the outside observing, detached and distant, but will have jumped over that unseen line that is the divider of the spectator and the spectated. And if I cross that line, which I am slowly realising I am in the process of doing, then I will find myself in a place called Acceptance where a sharp critical eye cannot function. I had suspected this was already happening to me when one of the school kids, on a week's work experience, was looking alarmed at the behaviour of an established visitor who believes lots of deep breathing and staring are the appropriate accompaniment to his speech pattern of barked out phrases.

'Och, don't mind him,' I assured her, 'that's just Mr Climont, he's really quite nice and very well read too.'

Oh dear. Yes, indeed, there is a major shift occurring in the ramparts of my mind. Conduct that I once perceived as nutty, bizarre, surreal, weird, peculiar, eccentric, strange, extraordinary, ludicrous, irregular, oddball, zany, left-field, freakish, wacky or just pure daft, has persistently eroded my once strongly fortified grasp of what is normal. I now take for granted, for example, that one customer will get seriously upset if we put his books in the bag with their spines facing upwards and another will be annoyed if his requested DVDs come with their titles delineated on the discs. Indeed I see this as quite normal. But what does that mean? Normal to whom, to what, to where? Perhaps what I am best settling for is that Cloisters offers a special kind of normal that is unique to its intrinsic self. The jury is still out though on whether or not it would ever achieve the status of 'ordinary' in my mind.

The other thing is that this book has to end somewhere and, if truth be told, it could run on and on. The stories, sketches and happenings will occur for as long as Cloisters remains open and hopefully that will be a long time yet. Whether or not I will remain until the final sale has been rung up is debatable. As I can already envision Kelvin's evaluation that my tales are 'scurrilous and irrelevant and idiotic and unwise' — with possibly a few more hundred other declamatory adjectives thrown in for good measure. I may decide that life could be quieter in another facet of the literary world. I may get fed up having to wear two pairs of leggings, two long sleeved close-fitting T shirts under at least another three layers of clothing for nine months of the year so to feel moderately warm in the shop. I may finally lose patience with a Frequent Flyer or find myself yelling 'No, we don't want your scabby books, they look like a dog's dinner and belong in a skip!' at some chanty-wrastler. I may find that I just get fed up with books … no, I retract that, some things are in one's bloodstream. But whatever the gods have in store for me I know this — such a job is / was sheer gift for the storyteller. Cloisters and all therein, I thank and salute thee.

My Scots — English Glossary

aboot: about

aff: off

affrontit: ashamed / embarrassed

afore: before

aifter: after

ain: one's own

airms: arms

amang: amongst

aroon: around

atween: between

auld: old

aw: all

aye: yes

aye hot: always hot

aye looked aifter: always looked after

back-chattin: talking back / objecting

baffies: slippers

bevelled: bent out of shape

blether: chat

bogey: trolley / cart

cannae: can't

caird: card

cairry: carry

cairry-on: high jinks / fun

caw canny: go carefully

cawd: called

chanty-wrastler: chancer

chield: fellow. *Can be used affectionately or contemptuously*

clamjamfrie: ragged crowd

clarty: dirty, muddy

cleek: link

cliver: clever

cludgie: toilet

confusit: confused

coudnae: couldn't

crabbit: tetchy, cross

cried: called / named

dae: do

daein: doing

daud: a clump / a fistful

deid: dead

didnae: didn't

dinna: don't

disnae: doesn't

dominie: schoolmaster

dook: dip / plunge

doon: down

douce: respectable

dug: dog

far ben: well in / a reverie

fechtin: fighting

fitba: football

flooer: flower

flyting: trading of insults

foostie: smelly / decayed

footer: awkward / also, 'to footer aboot' = to act in an aimless way

forbye: in addition to / apart from / beyond / except

fou: drunk

frae: from

freend: friend

fur: for

gaun: going

gie: give

git: got / get

glamourie: enchanted world

glisked: glanced / become fleetingly aware

gowan: daisy

gowk: fool

granweans: grandchildren

greet: cry

guid: good

guising: *The practice, especially at Halloween, of going from house to house in a masquerade offering entertainment in return for gifts or money*

haill: whole

hame: home

haver: to talk nonsense

hen: *familiar term of address for a girl or woman*

hermless: harmless

hid: had

hing: hang

hiv: have

hoose: house

intae: into

isnae: is not

ither: other

jalouse: guess / suspect / suppose

jile: jail

jist: just

jings: *mild expletive*

keek: surreptitious look

kenspeckle: well-known

liftit: lifted

lightsome: carefree, light of heart

ma: my

mair: more

masel: myself

manky: grubby

mibby: maybe

mindit: minded

mither: mother

moothie: mouth-organ

nae: no

naething: nothing

naw: no

noo: now

o'er / ower: over

oor: our

oot: out

ootside: outside

ontae: onto

oursels: ourselves

parritch: dish of oatmeal (or rolled oats) boiled in salted water

peelie-wally: pale, sickly, anaemic looking

perjink: prim, strait-laced

pieces: sandwiches

pinkie: little finger

pit: put

pit oot: (sense used in chapter 'Carriers and Couriers') to be annoyed

pit up: endured

poke: plastic, paper bag / envelope

prent: print

pu'd: pulled

quaich: a silver or pewter bowl-shaped drinking cup with two 'lugs' (ears) or handles

rin: run

roon: round

sae: so

sair: sore

schule: school

shot: a turn / a go (amongst other meanings)

skint: broke / penniless

skiving: not doing what you should be

skoosh: squirt

skoot: move quickly / point quickly

slaister: mess, confusion

sleekit: sly

sma: small

smeddum: gumption

spoilt: spoiled

spotit: spotted

startit: started

stooshie: clamour, argument, conflict

stourie: dusty

stovies: a hot dish of potatoes, onions and small pieces of meat

stramash: commotion / disaster

stravaig: aimless walk

swally: an alcoholic drink

swatch: a quick look / glimpse

swither: uncertain, indecisive

tackety: hobnailed

tae: to

tawtie: potato

telt: told / to direct, impart

information, with authority   youse: plural of 'you'

thae: those

thegither: together

the morra: tomorrow

thoat: thought

thrawn: obstinate, intractable

toon: town

tottie: small, minuscule

twinty : twenty

wabbit: tired

wan: one

wance: once

wantit: wanted

weans: children

wee: small

weel: well

wheesht: be silent

whit: what

whitever: whatever

wi / wae: with

wid: would

widnae: wouldn't

windae: window

wis: was

wisnae: wasn't

wrang: wrong

wummin: woman

wunner: wonder

wur: were

wurk: work

yersel: yourself

yin: one

Lightning Source UK Ltd.
Milton Keynes UK
UKOW05f0607241114

242077UK00002B/30/P